teach®
yourself

9-07

life begins at 50 – for women
bernice walmsley

For over 60 years, more than 50 million people have learnt over 750 subjects the **teach yourself** way, with impressive results.

be where you want to be
with **teach yourself**

For UK order enquiries: please contact Bookpoint Ltd, 130 Milton Park, Abingdon, Oxon, OX14 4SB. Telephone: +44 (0) 1235 827720. Fax: +44 (0) 1235 400454. Lines are open 09.00–17.00, Monday to Saturday, with a 24-hour message answering service. Details about our titles and how to order are available at www.teachyourself.co.uk

For USA order enquiries: please contact McGraw-Hill Customer Services, PO Box 545, Blacklick, OH 43004-0545, USA. Telephone: 1-800-722-4726. Fax: 1-614-755-5645.

For Canada order enquiries: please contact McGraw-Hill Ryerson Ltd, 300 Water St, Whitby, Ontario, L1N 9B6, Canada. Telephone: 905 430 5000. Fax: 905 430 5020.

Long renowned as the authoritative source for self-guided learning – with more than 50 million copies sold worldwide – the **teach yourself** series includes over 500 titles in the fields of languages, crafts, hobbies, business, computing and education.

British Library Cataloguing in Publication Data: a catalogue record for this title is available from the British Library.

Library of Congress Catalog Card Number: on file.

First published in UK 2006 by Hodder Education, 338 Euston Road, London, NW1 3BH.

First published in US 2006 by The McGraw-Hill Companies, Inc.

This edition published 2006.

The **teach yourself** name is a registered trade mark of Hodder Headline.

Copyright © 2006 Bernice Walmsley

Typeset by Transet Limited, Coventry, England.
Printed in Great Britain for Hodder Education, a division of Hodder Headline, 338 Euston Road, London, NW1 3BH, by Cox & Wyman Ltd, Reading, Berkshire.

The publisher has used its best endeavours to ensure that the URLs for external websites referred to in this book are correct and active at the time of going to press. However, the publisher and the author have no responsibility for the websites and can make no guarantee that a site will remain live or that the content will remain relevant, decent or appropriate.

Hodder Headline's policy is to use papers that are natural, renewable and recyclable products and made from wood grown in sustainable forests. The logging and manufacturing processes are expected to conform to the environmental regulations of the country of origin.

Impression number   10 9 8 7 6 5 4 3 2 1
Year   2010 2009 2008 2007

Thanks are due to the **teach yourself** team at Hodder for their friendly help and guidance and as always, I must thank my husband, William, for his continuing support, encouragement and patience.

acknowledgements

dedication

This book is for all the friends who have reached 50 along with (or in some cases before) me and are making the most of the opportunities this decade brings.

contents

01

introduction

In this chapter you will learn:
- why this decade is so important
- how to review your options
- that it's not too late to make changes.

In this practical guide to making the most of your 50s, you'll find plenty of guidance and help to get you through this challenging, but immensely rewarding decade of your life. People entering their 50s today are not old as their parents were at the same age. They are taking on challenges and grabbing life with both hands. Unfortunately, many people have very negative feelings about going into their 50s and see it as an end rather than a beginning. But, tackled with a positive attitude, entering your 50s can be – and should be – an exciting experience. Lots of choices are available to you and this book will help you, first to see these choices and then to negotiate your way through the choices and make the ones that will make the most of your 50s. Let's look at how you can maximize the enjoyment you will get from this exciting decade of your life...

Turning 50 and enjoying it!

When you reach 50 – as you probably have if you're reading this book – you're in your mid-life years. You're not at the end of your life or in your older years, as some people would have you believe. You've probably got a couple of decades or more of active life left to make the most of. If you want to make any meaningful changes in your life, now is definitely the time when you can do it. If you want to make a career change or travel more or study something you've always wanted to know more about, then you can do it now. If you leave it ten or 15 more years, you may not be as active as you need to be to make any radical changes and the time for major career moves will have passed. You will not have a sufficient number of active years left by that time to take full advantage of the benefits these changes can add to your life. Of course, like anyone of any age, you won't be able to walk straight into another job in a completely different field from the one you may be working in right now or to suddenly start travelling to exotic places without some preparation, but taken step-by-step, you will find that you can transform your life and get far more out of it than perhaps you thought possible when you were contemplating entering your 50s.

Your first step, if you decide you want to make some changes in your life, should be to consider just what you've got going for you. You haven't reached this age without gaining some valuable experience and this stage of your life brings with it some distinct advantages over people who are either much younger or much older. Consider these points:

- You've got plenty of active life ahead of you.
- You've earned some respect. People in mid-life have gravitas and are assumed to know what they are talking about. Younger people may need your help and advice.
- Older people will feel you've reached their level. They no longer view you as some 'whippersnapper' who doesn't know what she's talking about, but as someone to listen to. Not only do you appear to know your stuff and have experience of the world, but you also have the energy to follow through with your plans.
- You've got the experience to know your way around and you'll have the contacts. You've been meeting people as an adult for three decades or so and will now be able to make the most of knowing the right people.
- You're known in your local community. Hopefully, people will remember you when an opportunity comes up or you will hear 'on the grapevine' of things going on.
- You're probably more sexually confident than in your younger years. Sure, you might not have a figure that looks its best in a bikini but you know what's what and you know yourself. This leads to a better sex life.
- If life has gone roughly to plan so far, you'll have established a certain amount of financial security for yourself.
- You've got choices.

Now, we know that having choices and opportunities is not the end of the story. To make the most of all that is on offer to you in this wonderful decade of your life, you will need to be proactive and to make the right choices. If you want to make positive changes, you cannot just sit around waiting for life to come to you. If you do, the things that cross your path will be mostly problems. The menopause will come to you whatever you do, and family troubles – whether it is with the younger or the older members – will land on your doorstep without your intervention. The good bits that come without any effort will be few and far between – maybe a grandchild or two will arrive (but even then you will need to put some effort in to build up a satisfying relationship) or the odd tenner on the lottery will turn up, but everything else will require some input from you. You will need to go out and search out all the good things in life that are so abundant in your 50s and this book will help you to plan your campaign.

The various chapters in this book will guide you through making your plan to take advantage of all that this next decade has to offer and to make the changes in your life that you may be resisting. You will be able to deal with different areas of your life such as your job, your relationship, your parents and your children, your home and your health with the details found here.

First, we'll look at where you're at right now.

What you can – and can't – do now that you're 50

It is easy – and quite common – for people entering their 50s to believe that life must start to slow down at this stage, that opportunities are really meant for the young and won't come along for them now. They think that people in mid-life should not be looking for change and that what you've got is what you must settle for. But this is far from the truth. Sure, if you're happy with things as they are, you can carry on with it but mid-life is an absolutely ideal time for change, for making the most of opportunities and for taking some real action. There's no doubt that you will see some negative changes in your body in the next few years – if you haven't already – but you should still be capable of doing almost anything you desire. One of the things that you definitely can do in your 50s is to improve your fitness and to eat well. This is dealt with in some detail in Chapter 3 but, for now, simply believe that it is possible to make the very best of your body to ensure that it is as fit as possible for the life you want to lead. If you feel that you are getting sluggish as you get older, that you need to slow down, then improving your diet and increasing your activity levels could transform your life. A better diet – one that does not rely on processed foods, is low in sugar and salt and incorporates plenty of fresh fruit and vegetables – can make you feel energized. A brisk walk a couple of times a week and a session at the local swimming pool can put a spring in your step and leave you raring to go and make the most of yourself and your life. Some people take up exercise in their 50s, having done very little previously, and they are very successful. Experts give plenty of reasons why this is a good idea. By exercising, you can improve the quality of your life now and in the future. Now is the time to speed up – not slow down.

> **Top tip**
>
> Gyms and leisure centres often offer special rates and also classes for people over 50. If you have any medical condition that could be improved by exercise, your doctor may refer you to a local leisure centre at special rates.

In your 50s you can certainly face life with optimism. Of course, this is a state of mind but it is one that can be fostered. There are a number of things that can influence our ways of thinking and it is in mid-life that we need to be particularly careful that negative attitudes are not allowed to creep in. Take no notice of anyone who says that you must behave in certain ways when you're getting older or who thinks that you can't tackle new things in your life. Ignore all the magazines that give the impression that 20-somethings are responsible for all the good things happening in the world and that nobody else counts. These magazines feature fashion that caters for what seem like little girls to the average woman in her 50s and certainly don't ever have articles that bear any relation to her life.

> **Top tip**
>
> Find magazines that speak to you. There are plenty of magazines on the market now that feature positive articles about women over 50. They're far more realistic and encouraging than those featuring celebrities and skinny models.

Now that middle-aged women are becoming more forceful and a power to be reckoned with in society, there are magazines out there to serve the market and they feature successful, feisty women of all ages – all doing it for themselves. You might even get some inspiration from them.

Another thing that you can do to foster positive attitudes and ensure that you are ready to move on with this next phase of your life is to get your life in order. Declutter every area of your life – your home, your wardrobe, your job, your mind and your relationships – and life will become more positive and things will seem clearer. You may well find, after you have thoroughly decluttered your life, that you know what it is that you have to do. You might find that radical changes are needed at home or at work and you are in a position to take the first step towards change and a more rewarding life.

So, all those interesting, energising things are what you can do in your 50s, but what about the things you can't do? In actual fact, there are very, very few things that are not open to a woman in her 50s. She might not have the washboard-flat stomach of a 20-year-old or the speed of a 30-year-old but with perseverance and determination, she can do anything. She can retrain for most jobs, take extra qualifications, change careers, stay at home or go out to work, travel the world or start a business. What she can't do is pretend that she has all the time in the world to achieve her aims.

What you must not do is allow any drawbacks you have now that you're in your 50s to hold you back. If you have minor ailments that you either didn't have or that wouldn't have bothered you when you were a decade or two younger, then don't let them deter you now. Maybe you've started feeling a little achy in the mornings – doesn't it get better as the day goes on, when you get moving? So, get moving. Also, don't let guilty feelings or too much responsibility blight your life. Your life belongs to you, not to your children, or your partner or your parents. Sure, you will still have some responsibilities to other people but make sure that they are genuine responsibilities and that other people couldn't easily manage to do more for themselves. Above all, don't let attitudes hold you back – either your attitudes or those of other people. A positive, 'can-do' attitude at this stage in your life is an asset that can change your life. A negative attitude will push you sharply into old age and hold you there. I should perhaps make it clear here that contentment is not a negative attitude. If you're happy and satisfied with how your life is, then don't let anyone tell you that you must change. Stay where you are and enjoy it. But if there are areas that you want to change, be aware that you can change.

If you have any unrealized ambitions, now is the time to take the first step towards what you want. If you leave it for many more years, gnawing away at you, you will have missed an opportunity. If you want to achieve something, you should start now. So, lack of time left is the only limiting factor in the life of a woman in her 50s and this should spur you on to taking positive action – right now.

New age, new opportunities

This decade of your life is a time when you can make drastic changes to your life and get away with them. And not only get away with them, but still have plenty of time to enjoy them. Some people view the sudden desire for change in their 50s as a 'mid-life crisis'. But it needn't be a crisis – it all depends on your viewpoint. Try looking at your desire for change as an opportunity to make the most of your life and to make your dreams come true rather than as some sort of problem. With the ebbing of responsibilities (for children, mortgages and so on) the opportunities can flow. Your lack of financial and family ties can release your creative or carefree side so that all sorts of things become possible. We'll address some of the things a woman in her 50s might want to do – i.e. almost anything – and how she can make a start on them, in later chapters but for now just start to dream. Let your mind wander around and bring to the surface all the things that would enrich your life. Make sure that no negative thoughts about being too old or things not being appropriate intrude on this process. For now, anything goes.

Keep growing and changing: Jackie's story

It's never too late to change. A friend of mine, Jackie, left school at 16 with no qualifications and went into general office work – something her mother said would be just right for her. She's in her 50s now, so her first job was a few years before personal computers were in evidence. She prepared invoices manually, becoming very quick with figures and learning the basics of lots of areas of office work such as credit control, sales administration and stock control. She married and brought up two children, all the time contributing her modest salary to the family's finances. Despite her busy life she felt that she was capable of more, and when her children went to senior school she started to study for a degree with the Open University. She got her degree in the Arts and was very pleased with herself but still felt that something was missing. By this time her children were away at university and she was still working for a small local firm of stationery suppliers, running their office, while her husband had steadily climbed to a well-paid position in the firm he had started work with when he left school. She saw her opportunity for change when a friend told her that she was planning to open her own art gallery but needed a partner in the business. Her hopes were dashed initially by her husband's reluctance to invest money and to let go of the security that her small – but regular – wages afforded the family. He told her that women of her age didn't get involved in ventures like this. But this new venture became more and more important to her. She would be working in a field that really interested her and doing something for herself for possibly the first time in her life. The skills that she had acquired throughout her life would finally be appreciated. So she held firm and her husband could see he had no choice if he wanted his wife to be happy. She became a partner in the art gallery and eventually earned more than she had ever dreamed of, while enjoying her working life, making interesting friends and proving to herself – and everyone else around her – that she was capable of far more than expected. She had just needed the opportunity and the determination to make the most of it.

Summary

In this chapter, hopefully, you have been convinced that turning 50 is cause for celebration. You have seen how it is possible to change your life and grab your opportunities so that you make the best you can of the exciting decade that you are about to embark upon.

Action plan: reviewing where you are

Do a very quick SWOT analysis of where you are at now. If you've not done one before, this involves listing the Strengths, Weaknesses, Opportunities and Threats that exist for you right now. It will help you to see where you need to apply your efforts and will assist you with the plan that we will start to build up in the next chapter.

Here's an example of just such an exercise, completed by a woman aged 50, that should assist you in doing this for yourself:

Strengths	financial – mortgage paid off, high earnings
	physical – plenty of energy
Weaknesses	physical – weight too high, started the menopause a year ago

Opportunities	employment – considering self-employment
Threats	employment – lack of security
	relationship – spend very little time with husband
	family – father's health failing, may need full-time care in future

Take note of how this woman has considered various areas of her life and covered problems and advantages so that she will be in a position to see what needs to be done to make sure she enjoys her 50s.

02

planning your 50s

In this chapter you will learn:
- why you need to set goals
- how you can make time for yourself
- how to make the most of your 50s.

A great part of your planning as you enter your 50s will involve your financial arrangements for your retirement and, being such an important subject, this is dealt with in much more detail in Chapter 13. But what else will you need to plan?

Apart from dealing with family issues such as care arrangements for your parents and other elderly relatives and perhaps a wedding for your son or daughter, the other major area of your life that you will need to think about is your time. How will you spend your time during the next decade, when many of your family responsibilities will have lessened and maybe the heat has been taken off your career, freeing up time that you may not be used to? You may even have to plan for lots of free time if you will be taking early retirement. As we go through our earlier years, fighting to establish a career – with the long hours of working that this can involve – and getting ourselves on the housing ladder, then raising a family, we may not have to worry about how we use our free time as we may not have very much of it, so this can come as a bit of a shock in our 50s. So, it may take some thought and some planning. With 15 or 20 active years ahead, not all the things that you do with your time can be casual, leisure-time activities. You will need to plan to do some things with a purpose. Now is the time to bring to the front of your mind all those dreams and ambitions that you have had to put on hold while the family was growing up or while you were forging your way up your career ladder. Think about all the things you have wanted to do or learn. Maybe there are hobbies you've wanted to take up or changes you need to make to your appearance or your attitudes. Whatever you come up with, there will be an element of planning required to make sure that you fit them into your life and achieve just what you want to achieve. The first step is to set some goals.

Setting your goals

By now you should have realised that your goals can be anything. They might be related to fitness levels – perhaps you want to run a marathon or climb a mountain or maybe you just want to be fit enough to get out of your armchair without giving that 'old lady grunt' as you do so. Or you could have financial goals – perhaps you want to retire early or provide for your grandchildren's education. Or you could want to lose weight. Or you could simply want to enjoy life. Whatever your goals involve, you will have a much better chance of reaching them if you carefully define them, plan for them and write them down. Formalizing them in this way will make your goals seem so much more real. Your written goals will become promises to yourself.

Your goals must be real to you. They may be things that you have dreamed about for years or things that just pop into your head as you're starting to plan. One trick to making your goals seem more real and to bring them within your reach is to use visualization. If, for example, you want to go to Australia as a retirement gift to yourself, you should picture yourself on the plane, arriving at some of the more famous landmarks, walking around Ayers Rock or surfing on Bondi beach, tucking into a substantial barbecue meal and basking in the sun at Cairns. To make your visualisation task easier in this example you could collect a few brochures and do a bit of research on the Internet. Make sure that you put yourself in the picture – this is your goal and you must be part of it.

The most important thing to remember is to make your goals as specific as possible. Don't just say 'I want to lose weight'. It would be far better to say 'I am going to lose 10 pounds before my holiday in June'. If you set vague goals you will have difficulty knowing when you have achieved them and that will not do your self-confidence and motivation any good at all. But, I hear you say, what about those more vague things, many of which are about self-improvement – that are difficult to be specific about? Things such as wanting more self-confidence or being more motivated. There are two tricks you could use here to help you. First, you could rate yourself on the attribute you want to gain. If you've chosen increasing your self-confidence as a goal, give yourself a score on the scale of 1 to 10. Maybe you're a 3 or a 4 in the area of self-confidence just now. Where do you want to be – maybe an 8 or a 9? Then that will make your goal more specific. A second trick is to find ways that you will know that you have gained more self-confidence – perhaps you will walk into a room full of strangers without worrying about your appearance – and these ways will become parts of your goal.

Quick tips to boost your confidence

- Stand tall. Your posture will make others think you're more confident than you are and it will even fool you into feeling better about yourself.

- Try thinking about how others feel. Concentrating on yourself will allow you to find things to worry about if you are short on self-confidence. Others may feel just as uncomfortable as you do and if so, perhaps you can put them at their ease. Or they may actually be very self-confident people and if so, you might be able to learn how they do it.
- Avoid self-criticism. Making sweeping statements to yourself about your abilities or lack of them is rarely helpful, so ignore that critical inner voice.
- Keep challenging yourself. If you don't practise you won't improve, so make sure that you don't avoid social situations where your confidence is tested.
- Think positive thoughts. If you find yourself becoming anxious, remind yourself of a time when you felt great. Prepare a few examples of when things went right for you or when you felt really good about yourself so that you can use them when necessary.

Another thing to note is that your goals must be realistic. Setting a goal of becoming the head teacher of a large school when you're 55 and haven't even qualified as a teacher yet may not be possible. That's not to say your goals shouldn't be ambitious, but you must accept that some things – not all – have limits.

Your next step is to prioritize your goals. If you have a long list of things that you want to do and to achieve and changes you want to make, you will probably be looking at it thinking, 'This is impossible. Where do I start?' Well, you will start with the thing that's most important to you. The item at number one in your list. If you think everything is important, try asking yourself a few questions:

- What do I want most?
- What will make the greatest difference to my life?
- Are any of these goals duplicated? That is to say, by achieving one of them would you be on your way to achieving another?
- Are any of the goals on my list long-term ones that I should not be working on right now? For example, if one of your goals is to travel extensively in your retirement, this is a long-term goal if you know that you will not be able to retire for many years.
- Do any of my goals need resources that I do not yet have? If you want to take up golf with your husband but he is still working very long hours, tell him about your goal but don't put it at the top of your list just now.

Prioritizing is necessary because you must be careful not to overwhelm yourself. If you tried to do everything at once you probably wouldn't achieve much at all. So, now you must choose the top three or four goals to work on immediately. The others can be set aside to be dealt with in the future – probably when you have made some progress on the first batch of goals. Your next step is to break each goal that you have decided to work on into all the component steps. If your goal is to become self-employed, these steps might include brainstorming ideas, researching your competitors and the local market, writing a business plan (and that in itself could have various component parts – see Chapter 12 for more details), raising funding, marketing, buying materials, finding customers, finding premises, starting work, etc. Split your goal down into as many steps as possible – even very small steps – so that it becomes almost like a 'to do' list. You will then be able to get on with the task of working towards your goal and get plenty of satisfaction along the way from ticking things off your list.

Following these steps will ensure success and will mean that your life will undoubtedly change for the better. But, just in case you're thinking, 'Why bother with all this goal-setting business? I'll just get on with it, I know what I want really', then bear in mind that failure comes when we fail to plan. But success comes when you plan to succeed.

Who can help?

Deciding who can help you to reach your goals depends on what your goals are. If you want to start a business, for example, then a visit or phone call to your local Business Link will uncover lots of ways they can help. They have the low-down on business advice, training and financial help that may be available according to what sort of business you are thinking of starting. Your local Chamber of Commerce will also be a valuable source of help and, as ever, the Internet and your local library are good places to start your research. There will be more information about starting a business in Chapter 12.

If you're thinking of taking up some form of exercise then check out the facilities offered by your local council – they are often cheaper and less dominated by Lycra-clad (extremely slim) fitness fanatics. If you've got in mind a new hobby such as card making or oil painting then your local college will have information on courses available.

Whatever your goal may be, the people around you will often be your best source of help. Family and friends will often have experience of some aspects of what you are trying to achieve or, at the very least, can be a source of support and understanding if things don't always go to plan. They can also sometimes be enlisted to help if you are having difficulty in achieving your goals because you find it hard to keep going or tend to procrastinate. A trusted friend could be enlisted to call you every morning to check if you have done your 30-minute walk for the day if you're embarking on a programme of exercise – or they could join you in your campaign to get fit as it's always easier to keep going if you feel someone else is depending on you. Certainly if you are giving up a well-paying – but boring – job to pursue your dream of self-employment, you will need the full support of your partner. You will need to be sure that they are prepared to take on the full financial responsibility for your home and all the expenses to which they have been used to you contributing – discussions on this are vital, preferably before you let go of that salary.

> **Top tip**
>
> If you're going to have to live on a reduced income for a while as you start your business, try living on it during the run-up to giving up your job. Make the economies now and not only will you become used to them and see if they work but you can also add to your savings.

Challenge yourself

Don't let your goals be restricted by your perceptions of what you can and can't do. Sometimes these perceptions will be false. A belief that you are 'no good at talking to people' or 'hopeless at figures' may have been formulated in your childhood and no longer be true, but it may still stop you from pursuing your dreams. If one of your goals is to update your image, you could be seriously hampered by a conviction – established in your teens, three or four decades ago – that clothes in bright pink or longer skirts don't suit you. So, when you're setting your goals, review your self-perception at the same time. You may be surprised by what you find. If you find it difficult to be honest with yourself and to let some of these false perceptions go, enlist the help of a close friend or answer the following questions to give yourself a new way of thinking about yourself:

Re-assessing your self image

1 When you see pictures of slim young models in magazines, do you think:
   a) She's too thin.
   b) I wish I looked like her.
   c) It's all done with airbrushing.

If you answered (b) then you could maybe consider that a lot of airbrushing does go on in advertising photography and that most models probably are too thin. In reality, very few of us have any chance at all of looking like a model. After all, they're usually about 5'10" tall and in their teens. If you're 5'2" and in your 50s then clearly it's an impossible dream and if you know you can't be 5'10" then why is it reasonable to think you can be as thin as they are?

2 Next time you're walking along the street, look around you. Do you see:
   a) lots of women who are a lot slimmer than you
   b) ordinary women
   c) a mixture of fat women, thin ones, average ones...

If you replied (a), ask yourself if you also saw a lot of women who were fatter than you. If you didn't and only noticed the ones who are slimmer than you (or whom you think are slimmer than you – most of us have an image of ourselves as bigger than we actually are) then you need to be careful that you're not viewing the world in a way that gives you a false impression. In reality, the world is made up of all shapes and sizes and we should value our individuality. Worrying about what other people look like in comparison with ourselves is not going to allow us to enjoy life to the full.

3 When someone gives you a compliment about what you're wearing, do you say:
   a) What, this old thing? I've had it for years – and it was so cheap...
   b) Oh, I think it makes me look a bit fat, actually.
   c) Thank you, I've always liked this dress.

If you know you would answer (a) or (b) then ask yourself why you don't believe someone who says something nice about you. Why would they lie? Try to look at yourself through their eyes. It is probably a perfectly lovely dress that you look great in. Enjoy it!

4 In a discussion with a mixed group of friends, do you offer your opinion:
   a) never – it's probably wrong anyway
   b) hesitantly – all your friends are so much cleverer than you
   c) as much as you can – you enjoy a good exchange of opinions

If you answered (a) or (b) have a good look at your friends. Are they really all so much better qualified or knowledgeable than you? Or is it just your lack of confidence holding you back? Next time you're in this situation, think about what you feel about what is being discussed and be determined to give your opinion – and remember, your opinion is as valid as anyone else's.

5 You're considering applying for a new job. Do you:
   a) think, 'No, I'll stay where I am – better the devil you know...'
   b) not apply because you're sure you're not good enough
   c) go ahead: who knows where it may lead...

If you replied (a) or (b) to this last question, then you're obviously lacking in confidence in your abilities. But how do you know what you're capable of if you've never pushed yourself? How do you know who else will be applying for the job? You can't make a decision about your chances if, as in this case, you don't know who the competition will be.

Self image is about how we see ourselves. And sometimes we get it wrong. This little quiz should have helped you to understand that seeing yourself negatively is not helpful – try to remember this the next time you have doubts about your appearance, your opinions or your abilities.

A way in which many women in their 50s choose to test themselves is to take on a physical challenge such as a walk, a run or expedition for charity. This could range from running a marathon in aid of your chosen charity to climbing Kilimanjaro, trekking through Borneo or walking just a few kilometres. Events like this are run by various charities and you can find them by looking on your favourite charities' websites or in the national press. If you've been affected by illnesses such as breast cancer or diabetes then there will usually be some sort of physical challenge that will be held in aid of the charities and will give you what you need, at the same time as the feeling of satisfaction that comes from charity work. Some people take these challenges in their stride, while others wouldn't think for even a second that they are capable of the physical effort involved. Again, the important thing is to push yourself. Don't let inertia or your false perceptions stop you from putting some excitement back into your life. Of course, you will have to train for any of the big events but don't automatically think it's not for you. Check it out.

Becoming self-employed is another common challenge for women. Leaving behind the security of a regular salary and taking on the responsibility for a business, however small, is a major change but if it is for you, go for it.

A few words of caution here. Although you should certainly be challenging yourself in your 50s, your more ambitious goals should not be achieved at the expense of the other important things in your life. You need to allow yourself time to just be yourself. Time to relax and time to spend with the people who matter to you.

Making time for yourself

If you're going to take on challenges and work towards your goals as well as keeping everyday life going – perhaps you've still got a job to juggle with your remaining family responsibilities and a social life – then you will need to make some time for yourself. You will have to find the time to devote to your new hobbies and challenges. Managing your time will be something that you have probably had to get to grips with in your working life and, if you have brought up a family, time management will have been an invaluable skill. That same skill will come in handy now if you are wondering how you will be able to find the time to accomplish any of your goals. Of course, there will be times when you feel overwhelmed – and that's OK, everyone feels snowed under sometimes – but when the busy period passes, pick yourself up and get back to your goals. Determination will help you to succeed.

There are a few time management tips that can help with managing your time even on this informal basis:

- Make sure you know exactly what you currently spend your time on. If most of the things you do are essential and you cannot or do not want to ditch these tasks – for example, looking after your grandchildren or the minimum of housework – then you may have to be very strict with the things that you do that are not essential – shopping, watching television etc.

- Ask yourself if everything you do has to be done. Many of us carry on doing some tasks out of habit. We vacuum the carpet more frequently than is strictly necessary or keep entertaining our offspring instead of letting them have us round for a meal occasionally.

- Ask yourself if you are the best – or only – person for the job. Can your partner not take his turn and change the bed on alternate weeks? Or is there anyone to whom you could delegate some of the tasks concerned with caring for elderly relatives?

- Use a daily 'to do' list. Even if everything you do is concerned with leisure, home responsibilities and achieving your goals and you feel that you should not need to formally record this sort of task, do try keeping a list. Apart from it being very satisfying to tick the 'done' items off your list, you can also see at a glance where your time is going. You will then perhaps be able to eliminate some of the tasks if they seem less important when listed alongside those that will bring you closer to achieving your goals.

- Always break down tasks into smaller parts, just as you did with your goals. It not only allows you to see what needs to be done and how long it will take, but it also makes the whole thing seem more manageable.

The main thing to remember is that you are trying to make time for yourself. You may have spent your whole life making time for other people but now that you've reached your 50s, you must start to put yourself first and make sure that you have the time to enjoy the rest of your life.

Of course, it might be that you already have time to spare, having reduced your family responsibilities recently and maybe working shorter hours, and if that is the case then you will not need to worry too much – your time for yourself will have appeared as if by magic. Your task is to enjoy it by challenging yourself and achieving your dreams.

Apart from making time for yourself and to spend with friends and family, you must also make sure that you don't pursue your goals with such single-mindedness that you lose yourself in them. Prior to your goal-setting exercise you will have had a life that included, hopefully, many happy moments. Unless you're in need of some drastic changes and are aware of this need, you shouldn't change everything at once. Keep the best bits and nurture them.

Top tip

The most important thing is to enjoy this time in your life – so don't try to fill every second of your life with goal setting and chasing unfulfilled ambitions. Acknowledge when things are great for you.

This brings us to an exercise that can – and should – be done alongside your goal setting and will bring this chapter on successful planning for your 50s to a close. For the sake of your long-term happiness and contentment you need to know what matters to you and then these things can be linked in to your goal setting. It is a way to learn a lot about yourself. Why not make a list now:

- What makes you happy? It may be small things such as baking a cake, dinner with friends, running a mile in your personal best time, paying off your mortgage, being able to help out your children or family gatherings. Think of the things that make you smile. Do not make the mistake of thinking that money makes you happy – certainly it helps, but it is the things that money can give you such as security, family holidays or a comfortable home that will increase your happiness.

- Count your blessings. Presumably you've got a roof over your head, can read and write and have sufficient food to eat. If so, you're luckier than the majority of the world's population. You will also have other things to be grateful for such as a loving partner, healthy children or good friends. List all of these things.

- Who are you? Are you living a life that makes you feel true to yourself? Every one of us has talents and strengths and it is when you are using these that you will feel most satisfied. Think what you were doing when you last felt really happy with yourself. What do you – and the people around you – see as your 'signature strengths'?

- What could you not live without? This can be people or pets, your home or a possession or two.

- Make sure you've covered all the different areas of your life – include family and friends, work, leisure time, your spiritual side plus time for looking after your health.

The list you end up with after this last exercise will guide you towards all the things that matter to you and should form a central part of your life, be incorporated in your goals and in how you spend your time in your middle and later years.

Summary

In this chapter you have done a lot of work on finding out just what you will be doing with your time in your 50s. If you have followed each of the sections you will now have a set of goals – things that you want to achieve in the next decade or two of your life (and if you haven't got your goals totally sorted out yet, carry out the action plan that follows this summary). By now you should be excited and raring to go, having set goals that matter to you and found out where you will find the time to devote to these things.

Action plan: where do you want to be and how will you get there?

Now is the time to commit yourself to taking action. If you are serious about making the most of this fabulous decade of your life – and the decades that follow it – you must know what you want and how you are going to achieve it. If you have a vague desire to better yourself in some way but never clarify your thoughts and never get a plan together, you will get nowhere. So, remembering your strengths, weaknesses, opportunities and threats that you listed during Chapter 2, sit down with a piece of paper and write down the following:

- What you want to achieve. This is the most important of your goals. You may have lots of things you want to do but in this exercise we are concentrating on just one – make it one that is really important to you. Be specific. Make sure that you write down a realistic timeframe for this goal and that you go into plenty of detail so that you will be in no doubt when you have achieved the goal. What do you expect to see? What changes will take place? How will you feel?

- What you need to do to make your dreams come true – write this down in as much detail as possible, including what resources you will need and how you will put these resources in place. This encompasses the time, effort, money, support from others and anything else you will need to ensure success.
- What is the first step you need to take?

Now, take that first step and you will be well on your way to making your 50s the best time of your life.

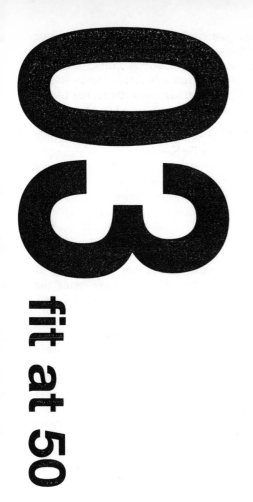

03

fit at 50

In this chapter you will learn:
- how the ageing process affects us all
- how to set realistic exercise goals
- how to eat a healthier diet.

Getting older is inevitable – we can't stop it but we can turn it from a possible disaster into a very acceptable part of life. The key to ageing well is keeping fit and active. Of course, there are diseases and genetic conditions that can affect your fitness levels, and there may be little you can do about these, but fitness is usually a matter of choice rather than chance. The choices you make now will affect the type of old age you make for yourself. If you choose to sit in a chair thinking you're too old to change now, or keep resolving to join a gym but never getting round to it, or ordering another take-away meal and settling down for yet another night in front of the television, or driving to the shops that are only a ten-minute walk away, or helping yourself to another giant piece of chocolate cake, then you may be storing up trouble for yourself in later years. If, on the other hand, you choose to take a brisk walk every day, or to work at changing your diet into a healthy one, or to take action and join that gym now, or to take up a hobby that will make you active, such as cycling or badminton or tennis, then you will have made the right choices. You will be on your way to a healthy and rewarding old age.

Let's look at the consequences of making the wrong choices. Imagine yourself in 20 or 30 years. If you've led a life with little or no exercise, have overeaten and neglected your body for years then, if you reach old age, you will almost certainly be leading a life of limited possibilities. You may be sitting in a chair all day – from when you get up to when you go to bed, and then only able to get up with help. Someone may have to help you to the toilet, prepare all your meals and even feed them to you, wash you and dress you. You may not be able to go outside very often because it takes too much effort. You may have to look on as others lead their lives. Your relationships with your children and grandchildren may suffer, as you are so dependent on them for every little thing. You won't be much fun for your grandchildren and great grandchildren to be with because you can't do anything. There will be no games of football or even strolls in the park with them if you can't move around with ease. Life will be pretty dull.

Top tip

Don't get too carried away with improving yourself. One bar of chocolate or staying inside watching TV on a rainy day won't ruin all your efforts to get fit. What matters is what you do for the majority of your time.

Keeping yourself fit and active is essential in your 50s if you want to lead a worthwhile life in your later years. It will also make life a lot easier and more rewarding right now, so it is well worth putting in the effort. It will almost certainly be an appreciable effort though, as it becomes more difficult – for all sorts of reasons – to gain or maintain an acceptable level of fitness, as we get older. We'll check out these reasons in the next section.

Why you have to work harder: the technical stuff

The natural ageing process, ranging from loss of muscle to deteriorating digestive processes will cause changes in your level of fitness and health by the time you get into your 70s. Most of the effects of this process can be improved by keeping yourself active and at the correct weight for your height in your earlier life. The unpalatable truth, however, is that keeping fit gets more difficult as we get older simply because we are not only working our bodies but also because we are fighting against these natural ageing processes. Let's look at some of the physical effects of getting older:

- Loss of muscle – by the time we reach 80 we will have lost anywhere from 20 to 60 per cent of our muscle mass. Women who do not do any exercise will be at the top end of this loss. To keep this loss to a minimum we need to stay as active as possible throughout our lives. One of the effects of loss of muscle mass is a slowing down of movement.
- Slower metabolism – this is another effect of loss of muscle. Muscles burn more energy than fat so, if we don't reduce our calorie intake, we will inevitably gain weight.
- An increase in body fat – we will gain up to ten pounds of body fat per decade as we age. With increased weight comes the increased risk of obesity-related problems such as diabetes, high blood pressure, strokes and heart disease.
- Loss of strength – if we lose muscle mass then our strength decreases accordingly.
- Getting shorter – poor posture and spinal deterioration cause us to lose height as we age. We can expect to lose up to six inches of our normal adult height by the time we reach 80 years of age.
- Loss of bone density – this affects everyone but is more pronounced in women than in men. A woman might lose up

to 30 per cent of her bone density by the time she reaches old age. This will cause fractures to happen as a result of even relatively minor accidents and is one of the causes of loss of height as detailed above.

- Changes in the digestive system – our digestive juices decrease as we age and this can make it more difficult to obtain all the nutrients from our food that we need in order to stay healthy.
- Deteriorating vision and hearing – eyes and ears wear out and do not function as well in our later years as they did when we were young.

Just reading about all of these changes can be disheartening but all is not lost. You can do something to improve the state of your body as you age. True, you will never be able to regain the slim, smooth body that looked good in a bikini when you were in your 20s. You probably won't be able to run as fast or as far as when you were much younger. And you might not be as strong as you once were. But you can keep the effects of ageing to a minimum if you can develop – and stick to – a fitness routine that gets your heart beating faster on a regular basis, is weight-bearing and increases your flexibility. That's the good news to follow the bad news. It is perfectly possible to change our habits, in terms of how active we are and what we eat, to the point that we can prevent the onset or progress of many of the detrimental effects of old age on our bodies. Even if there are effects that we cannot change or avoid, with a fit body we will be able to manage them to a much greater degree than if we are struggling with a rapidly deteriorating, overweight body. Our well-being in old age depends upon our attitude and actions now, in our 50s. Now is the time to do something that will ensure a fit old age. The next section will deal with how you can develop a routine and work to goals that suit you.

Realistic exercise goals

If you're feeling bored at this point and are convinced that you can't get fit because you don't like exercise or don't have the time to incorporate it into your life, please don't stop reading. Every 50-year-old is able to make improvements to their health and well-being. And every one of them certainly should. Just take another look through the list above of all the things that will deteriorate as we get older. Now try to imagine your life if – or when – all these things happen to you. Do you really want to allow your muscle mass to disappear to the extent that you won't be able to carry a bag of shopping or lift your grandchild? Do you want to struggle to get out of your chair because you're carrying so much excess weight around your middle? Do you want to risk heart disease that could shorten or severely limit your life? No, of course you don't, so what do you have to do to avoid or control these problems and how can you realistically manage your fitness? Initially, you should aim to:

- increase muscle mass by doing some simple strength exercises
- improve your cardiovascular capacity by taking exercise such as cycling, swimming or jogging
- increase bone density by taking weight bearing exercise such as walking or running – be careful here if you have a history of osteoporosis; check with your GP first
- improve your flexibility with a few stretching exercises or maybe taking a regular yoga class
- improve your diet – there is more about this in the next section.

Although activity levels among the over 50s are currently very low – it is estimated that 4 out of 10 people over 50 take no exercise at all – it is never too late to start your get-fit campaign. Being active doesn't just mean fending off illness. 'Being active improves the quality of life, it's not just about disease prevention,' says Bob Laventure, Consultant at the British Heart Foundation's National Centre of Physical Activity and Health at Loughborough University. 'There are a range of benefits from exercise in later years, such as improvements in the quality and quantity of sleep. It also helps digestion and by being active, you'll be getting out, meeting people and staying in your social network.'

There are yet more benefits to be had. 'All of us face up to eight dependency years at the end of our lives,' says exercise guru Dr Dawn Skelton. 'Exercising can reduce that time substantially. It helps to improve quality of life and lessen anxiety and depression.'

All this is easier said than done and determination and discipline are necessary to ensure your success. The best way is to start small. You don't necessarily have to rush out and join a gym, resolving to spend your every free moment there or to buy a full set of sports clothing, weights and rackets. The start of your healthier lifestyle can be a much simpler and cheaper affair than that. Look again at the list of things that you need to do and take them one by one. For example, you can improve your bone density – and most likely lose a bit of weight if you need to – by simply taking a brisk, 20-minute walk every day. Or you could incorporate more activity into your day – take the stairs instead of the lift when you're at work or in a big department store, for example, or walk to the local shops instead of taking the car. All of these things are completely free and are easy to get started on – all you need is determination and discipline.

Eating better

Eating a healthy diet is important at every stage of our lives. Eating a varied diet that includes carbohydrates, protein, fats, vitamins and minerals every day is vital for a properly functioning body and mind. Controlling the amount of protein, fats and carbohydrates we eat is necessary to ensure that we do not become overweight – or even obese. As we've seen previously, obesity is an attributed cause of a variety of life-limiting conditions including high blood pressure, diabetes and heart disease. This is especially true when we get to 50 and beyond, when our metabolic rate slows down. We may also become less active and have more time and money to eat out at fancy restaurants. The end result is that awful phrase 'middle-age spread'. There is no doubt that women's shapes change as they go through the menopause. Prior to the menopause they will have stored their excess fat mainly on their hips but with the hormone changes that take place at this time they start to store their fat around their middles – just as men do.

Top tip

Get to know the labels of food you regularly buy. There are various labelling schemes in operation – some state contents in great detail, some use a traffic light system (red to avoid, amber for eat in small amounts and green for eat freely).

So, what can we do to avoid getting overweight and ensure that we eat a healthy diet? Keeping our fat intake down will help – a woman of 50, weighing about ten stone, with average activity levels can maintain her weight on 2,300 calories per day. Higher activity levels or a higher starting weight will allow her to consume more calories. Changing our eating habits totally can be difficult, but simply exchanging some foods (the ones that contain very little nutritional value) for others (those with lots of nutrients) can be an inexpensive and easy way to start. Try substituting foods of high nutritional value for those with little:

substitute	*for*
steamed, grilled or baked fish	fried fish
olive oil	lard or butter
low fat yoghurt	creamy desserts
fruit	sugary snacks

When you've got those changes well incorporated into your daily meals and have probably lost a few pounds, you can then go on to reform the rest of your diet. At this point you can make sure that you incorporate a few things that will actively help your body to resist the signs of ageing. These six 'star foods' include:

1 Low fat dairy products – skimmed or semi-skimmed milk, low fat cheeses and spreads and yoghurts to ensure a plentiful supply of calcium. Calcium is essential for bone health and, with the prevalence of osteoporosis in older women, is especially useful for this group.

2 Whole grains – these can be dealt with by simply changing the type of bread you eat on a daily basis to wholemeal or granary bread and by ensuring that you eat a breakfast including a high fibre cereal such as bran flakes or porridge oats.

3 The onion family – eat onions, garlic and leeks several times a week. They contain antioxidants that can help to protect us from cancer and heart disease as well as the general ageing process.

4 Blueberries – these have, in recent years, come to be looked upon as a superfood. They have such high levels of antioxidants that they can stimulate the brain and help that failing memory.

5 Oily fish – salmon, trout, fresh tuna (the tinned sort loses its omega-3 properties) and mackerel should be incorporated into your diet twice a week. This will supply sufficient omega-3 oil to help us fight disease and help our hearts, joints, arteries and brain to function properly.

6 And finally, a glass of red wine. This has been shown to increase longevity due to its high antioxidant levels. But remember, it should be enjoyed in moderation – perhaps a glass a day.

Of course, to lose weight you must eat less, but starvation doesn't work, so you must eat a healthy diet. At the same time you will need to increase your activity levels. If you can do those two simple things on a regular basis, you will certainly lose weight and become healthier. You will be guaranteeing yourself a fitter, more useful old age.

It has been found that older people's diets are often deficient in calcium and certain vitamins but if you eat a wide variety of foods including those mentioned above, you will be getting all the nutrients you need. Calcium, as we have seen, is to be found in dairy products and, if you're keen to lose a bit of weight, there are very acceptable low-fat versions available. Other valuable sources of calcium include leafy green vegetables and tofu. Vitamins that you may be short of include Vitamins B12 and D. Vitamin D, which helps with the absorption of calcium, is produced in our skin when we're exposed to sunlight. As many older people become housebound, this can become a problem, but a supplement such as cod liver oil capsules can supply your needs. At least we baby boomers no longer have to take cod liver oil by the spoonful as I can remember doing in my childhood – and hating it. Vitamin B12 is found in fish, pork, beef, lamb, dairy products and eggs and helps to improve our concentration and memory as well as maintaining the nervous system.

Bearing in mind the above recommendations, we can now build up a suitable plan for healthy eating that would include, on a daily basis:

Breakfast	High-fibre cereal and fruit juice
Lunch	A sandwich made with two slices of wholemeal bread plus tuna with a salad.
	A low-fat yoghurt
Dinner	A piece of chicken or fish – grilled or baked
	A baked potato or some new potatoes boiled in their skins
	Two vegetables such as carrots and broccoli
	A glass of wine
	A bowl of blueberries or other fruit
Snacks	Have two snacks a day consisting of fruit or oatcakes with some low-fat cottage cheese
Liquids	Make sure that you drink plenty of fluid, especially water, during the day

This is a relatively easy diet plan, but if eating in this way is a long way from where you are now, don't despair. Take it one step at a time. Be determined to change your diet for the sake of your old age. Even if you've been eating junk – and lots of it – for most of your life, there is still time and opportunity to change. It is still worthwhile. If you can reduce your weight now, while you're in your 50s, and increase your activity too, you will be laying the foundations for a happier, healthier old age.

How to break your bad habits

Breaking old habits is never easy but, if the end result is a fitter body now and the hope of an easier and healthier old age, then surely it is worth the effort. Habits are formed over time and if you have developed bad habits – ones that have made you unhealthy – then you need to develop new ones to take their place. A habit can be established by doing something often enough and the key is to carry out your new way of eating and exercising as many times as it takes to create new habits that you will follow almost without thinking. So, for example, if you walk to the shop to buy a newspaper every day for a few weeks instead of driving there, you will eventually not even consider getting into the car for the trip to the newsagent. Here are a few tips to help you to stick to your new eating and fitness regime:

Eating habits

- Keep a diary. Write down everything you eat. You may be surprised by just how much food you eat. Take note too, of when you eat things. This should show you just what the problem is.
- Note your feelings when you're eating too much. If it's when you're stressed at work or bored or need comfort then that is the problem that needs to be solved.
- Keep busy. If you find that you tend to snack when you're bored – when you sit down in the evening to watch television or find yourself with a spare hour or so on a rainy Sunday afternoon – make sure that you've got something to do that will keep your hands busy. It's so easy to demolish a pile of chocolates without noticing while watching your favourite soap opera but more difficult if you're trying to complete some sort of craft project. It's almost impossible to eat much while you're making a batch of Christmas cards or knitting a

sweater for a grandchild or making a delicate item of jewellery.

- Keep motivated. Remind yourself just why you're trying to improve your diet. Are you thinking about your old age and planning for it to be healthier and happier by making sure that you're feeding your body with the right food? Or are you also trying to lose weight for the health and appearance benefits that will bring you. Whatever your motivation, keep it in mind. Visualise yourself as slim and happy or sprightly in your old age or happily playing games with your grandchildren without worrying about the physical effort required.

Exercise habits

- You should check with your doctor before commencing any programme of exercise and/or diet change especially if you have any health problems or have not exercised for a long time.
- Choose something you enjoy. If you used to enjoy tennis at school but haven't played much since, arrange some lessons for yourself. Book them and pay for them then you will have to at least try it out.
- Go on a fact-finding mission – to the nearest gym. If you think you don't like gyms, that they're not for you because they will be full of young girls in Lycra outfits then you must pay one a visit. You will probably find a wide cross-section of people there. There will be thin people and fat people including lots of older women wearing loose-fitting, comfortable clothing. While you're there, check out the programme of classes. Now, isn't there even one that you fancy?
- Get into a routine. Habits only become habits when you've completed an action about 20 or 30 times, so plan an activity into your day and do it for three weeks every day. There you are – a new habit.
- Get together with friends to exercise. If you make arrangements with friends to meet up for a game of badminton, for example, you'll find it much more difficult to sit back in your chair thinking 'I can't be bothered'.
- Get moving. The effect of exercise on the brain makes you feel good.
- Fool yourself. If you think that you hate exercise, forget exercise. Call it 'moving around' when you go up and down the stairs a couple of times extra each day. Or say you're just

'doing some chores' when you walk to the supermarket or the post office. You could even try to remind yourself that you're doing your bit for the environment when you leave the car at home and walk a mile or two.

- Broaden your view of 'exercise'. You don't have to go to a gym to get some exercise. One of the best forms of exercise to keep you fit well into old age is walking and this is easy because you can vary the length and speed and you don't need special equipment. But don't stop there. Any movement will help your fitness levels so clean the windows or polish the furniture, run up and down the stairs a few times or do some gardening. It all counts.
- Start slowly. Just plan to do five or ten minutes of exercise. Get past the barrier of those first few minutes and you probably won't be so desperate to stop.

Remember that the two things – dieting and activity levels – are inter-related, and that you'll get maximum benefits in terms of your health if you make an effort to improve both. The more activity you do, the less time you will have to sit and eat and the less you eat the more active you will want to be.

Looking your best

It can be disheartening at 50 to look at your body and realise the truth of all the changes that have taken place. Almost certainly your body shape will change during the menopause and if you've previously had a well-defined waist or been proud of your hourglass figure or washboard-flat stomach, you might not even recognize the body as yours. Your face will have gained a few wrinkles and your skin may have lost the dewy look typical of young girls. If you also have pretty, young daughters this will emphasize the changes you've been through and will undoubtedly make you feel worse about your own appearance. Learning to accept change is hard but has to be done. Nevertheless, we can all still make the best of ourselves. Try concentrating on these five areas of rewarding improvement:

1 Get some sleep

A good night's sleep will allow your skin to repair itself and let your major organs get on with the work of hormone production and renewing cells. A lack of good quality sleep will soon show in your face. Your skin will look dull and tired – not what you want if your aim is to look young and fresh.

2 Look after your skin

The most important thing you can do for your skin is to protect it from the sun. Use a moisturizer with a high sun-protection factor every single day. Sun damage will certainly result in dryness, wrinkles, age spots and patchy skin but it may also result in skin cancer so it is well worth making the effort to protect your skin from the sun. Of course, most of us feel better with a glowing tan but the best way to get it is out of a bottle or tube. Great strides have been made in recent years by the cosmetics companies and fake tans are now very effective and indistinguishable from the real thing. The only difference is that you aren't risking cancer to get it.

The usual skin-care advice of 'cleanse, tone and moisturise' applies particularly in your 50s. There are plenty of products on the market aimed at the mature woman but you will need to experiment a little to find just what suits you. There is no doubt that as we age, our skin changes. It becomes drier so we can usually abandon the treatments for spotty or greasy skin that may have suited us when we were younger and substitute a richer moisturiser and night cream.

3 Review your hair

A good cut and colour can take years off you. Don't stick to the same style for years unless you – and your hairdresser – are sure nothing else would look as good. Ask your stylist what might suit your hair type and face shape. Something as simple as cutting a fringe into your style when you've not had one before can really change your look – and just think of that wrinkled forehead it could be hiding. As we age, our skin tone changes, so make sure that your hair colour changes too. It might be that a few highlights to blend in the almost inevitable grey will be all you need to add or you may consider a completely different look. One thing's for sure, what looked great at 20 will not look so good now, so go to your hairdresser with an open mind.

4 Look after your teeth

Not only will you smile less if you are not confident with your teeth (and a miserable face is so ageing) but also missing teeth will cause your face and mouth shape to change. Cosmetic dentistry including implants and whitening treatments can make a difference to the general look of your face so consider what treatment, if any, you need. At the very least, regular visits for check-ups and a meticulous approach to cleaning your teeth will help to ensure that you keep your teeth well into old age.

5 Stand up straight

Poor posture can shout 'old woman' so put your shoulders back and stand tall. Slouching doesn't just look bad, it can also cause damage to our insides by putting pressure on our internal organs. Consider Pilates or yoga classes or at least some stretching exercises to help you to keep the youthful-looking posture of a younger woman.

Paying attention to just these five things can help to ensure that we look young and feel young while making the very best of what we've been given by way of looks, health and body type. There's no point in wishing for the body or skin of a young girl – that isn't going to happen – but an attractive 50-year-old woman who has confidence in her appearance and her abilities, who has experience that can't even be imagined by a 20-year-old, can look every bit as good.

Looking good in mid-life – some examples

These days a woman in her 50s who looks good is not a rarity. There are any number of celebrities who are 'well-preserved' – just think of Anna Ford, Lulu, Angela Rippon, Jane Seymour, Annie Lennox or Joanna Lumley, all of whom are over 50. And don't even think about Joan Collins – who is over 70! All of these women are not just attractive and looking younger than their years, they also have attitude. A positive view on life that shines out and adds to their beauty. Of course, you may be thinking that with the money these women must spend on their beauty routines and clothing, they certainly should look good, but impressive looks in mid-life are not limited to celebrities. Look around you – aren't there lots of ordinary women who are in their 50s who look great? For sure we all look younger now than our mothers did at our age, but 50 used to be old, really old. Now it is just the start of a new phase in your life. And it's an attractive phase in all respects.

Summary

- The key to ageing well is keeping fit and active.
- Poor diet and lack of exercise in our 50s can seriously affect the quality of life we can expect in old age.
- Ageing has many effects on our bodies including loss of bone density, a slower metabolism, loss of strength and muscle and an increase in body fat.
- Make exercise a daily part of your life.
- Make changes to your diet to counteract the changes caused by ageing; incorporate the six 'star foods' into your diet – low-fat dairy, whole grains, onions, blueberries, oily fish and the occasional glass of red wine.
- Look after just five things to make the most of your appearance – sleep, skin, posture, teeth and hair.

Action plan: get fit and stay fit

The key to getting fit and staying fit is to make exercise part of your routine. Give yourself time – say, a month – to form the exercise habits that will ensure that you are as fit in your 50s as you can possibly be and to pave the way for a healthy and active old age. The purpose of taking up exercise is to combat the natural effects of ageing and to build your stamina and flexibility so that you will be able to deal with whatever life brings. You must mix and match the things that you do to get fit so that they fulfil this purpose. An ideal combination of exercise will look after your bones and your heart and improve your flexibility. So, choose a mixture from the following:

Cardiovascular strength walking, cycling, swimming, tennis, badminton, dancing, gym work on a treadmill, cross trainer or rowing machine or even housework or gardening. Anything that makes you build up a slight sweat and makes you a bit breathless will be helping your cardiovascular fitness.

Flexibility the ideal exercise to improve and maintain your flexibility is yoga. You can attend local classes for this (and it is the safest way to start) but you can also get books, videos and DVDs to use at home. Yoga is also especially beneficial in that it can help you to relax and this will help to lower blood pressure and avoid stress. You could also do stretching exercises at home or any jobs – such as window cleaning, vacuuming and so on that involve bending and stretching.

Maintain bone mass this needs weight-bearing exercise such as walking, running or dancing. Anything where you move and are on your feet will help but the ideal way to start if you have not exercised much before is by walking. Start slowly – perhaps ten minutes a day – then build up. Aim for 30 minutes of walking, three or four times a week.

The three important things to remember about exercise are:

- you need a variety of types of exercise to ensure that you deal with all the effects of ageing
- you should enjoy it; choose something from each section that you know you will enjoy and then get on with it
- if it hurts, stop; take things gradually and you will get there.

And that's it. Simple. If you take up regular exercise, choosing a combination from the suggestions above, you will get fitter and be looking after some of the things that deteriorate as we get older.

To keep fit all you need to do is to keep it up. Get into a routine and keep going and you will stay fit and be able to deal with all that life throws at you.

04

health issues

In this chapter you will learn:
- ways to deal with the menopause
- how you can increase your chances of avoiding breast cancer
- how you can help yourself to stay healthy in your 50s.

There is no doubt that health issues make more of an impact on a woman's life when she enters her 50s than at any other time of her life. With the menopause comes a host of issues – all the side effects such as hot flushes, weight gain and so on, loss of bone density and the increased risk of heart disease – while for some women the loss of the chance to increase or start a family is a major concern. There are also the health problems that come to both sexes in their later years to worry about such as loss of strength and flexibility, arthritis, rheumatism and a slowing down of mental agility. Many of these things can be improved or even delayed by eating a well-balanced, healthy diet and taking a reasonable amount of exercise, as we saw in the previous chapter, but some issues will need dealing with in other ways and we will look at two of these – the menopause and breast cancer – in more detail next.

Changes – and the Change

As we've already seen, ageing brings with it lots of changes. As well as the health changes such as loss of muscle and bone and increased body fat, there are lots of positive changes such as the confidence that often comes with maturity, the financial security that can accompany middle age and the lessening of responsibilities for children. But, for women, there is one very important change – commonly known as 'the Change' – that usually comes along at around the age of 50. The menopause is the time when menstruation becomes less frequent and eventually stops. That's the positive bit – no more inconvenience every month and no more worry about getting pregnant. Unfortunately, for many women there are lots of negative aspects too. The most common problem is the onset of hot flushes and these can then happen over a period of months or years and can range from a mild irritation to a severe impairment of a woman's daily life. Other common symptoms include mood swings, night sweats, sleeplessness (often caused by night sweats), facial redness, thinning hair, dryer skin, weight gain, loss of libido, vaginal dryness and lack of concentration. That's a pretty awful list of symptoms but fortunately very few women, if any, experience all of these things.

There are plenty of choices as to how to deal with the inconvenience of menopausal symptoms. Some women are lucky enough to be able to ignore their symptoms, others take hormone replacement therapy (HRT), while others try supplements such as Soya, dong quai, black cohosh, red clover, sage or wild yam to combat the symptoms. We'll look at these in a little more detail later in this chapter.

While considering the efficacy of the various remedies available, do not overlook the importance of diet and lifestyle in dealing with the menopause.

Having the right attitude towards the 'change of life' – as with anything else associated with getting older – is certainly something that helps. Being determined to carry on with life regardless of the menopause and leading a happy and fulfilling life can go a long way to making the transition – from young, fertile woman to a woman past her childbearing years – a smooth and happy one.

Weight and where it is

One of the more unfortunate effects of ageing in women is an increase in weight with a corresponding change in body shape caused by where the extra weight is stored. Most women will find that their shape changes from the traditional pear shape, where any extra weight is carried on the bottom half of their body (or, if they were lucky in their younger years, an hourglass shape), to an apple shape, where extra weight is deposited around their middle. The waist becomes far less pronounced and it becomes more difficult to lose weight. The reason for this is thought to be that, with the body's loss of oestrogen from the ovaries at this time, it lays down fat as an oestrogen 'production unit' to compensate and, of course, when the fat is established, the body does not want to let the new oestrogen source go and hangs on to the fat.

Who can help?

There are three main sources of help for a menopausal woman who is struggling with the symptoms – her GP, a health food shop and her friends.

Your GP

A doctor should be a first port of call for a woman who suspects (or is depressingly certain) that she is going through the menopause. Confirmation that the menopause is indeed the reason for the symptoms being experienced is the first thing that the doctor will be able to do as well as give advice about coping with the menopause. He or she will be able to discuss the pros and cons of taking HRT and the suitability in individual cases. He or she may also be able to recommend alternative supplements and remedies.

Health food shops

The place for alternative remedies is the health food shop and many owners of such shops can be extremely helpful and knowledgeable about what they are selling. Do remember, though, that they are in business to sell you something, so do your research before you buy. Books, magazines and the Internet are good sources of information about supplements. The next section will start your research with a little information about the various remedies that you will no doubt find along the shelves of your local health food store.

Your friends

Friends can be a vital source of help and support in middle age and especially in dealing with the problems and changes brought about by the menopause. If you can talk openly to people you know and trust about the feelings and problems you may be experiencing, you will find that you will get, in addition to a healthy dose of sympathy and understanding, advice, recommendations for remedies and plenty of tried and tested knowledge. Simply knowing that you are not the only one to be having these problems can be enormously helpful too.

Managing your symptoms

If you've decided not to take hormone replacement therapy for any reason (more about HRT later), but are having menopausal symptoms that cause you problems in your daily life, you will want to try to manage these symptoms so that their effects are minimized. There are plenty of things that you can do for each of the different symptoms you may be experiencing:

Hot flushes and sweats

- keep your bedroom cool
- wear cotton next to your skin
- keep your bath or shower water cool or lukewarm rather than hot
- have a small fan handy to cool you down
- limit the number of hot drinks you have
- note whether any particular foods or drinks – especially spicy ones and alcohol – trigger hot flushes for you and keep them to a minimum
- if you're having real problems, talk to your doctor again. There are non-hormonal drugs such as Clonidine that may help you without incurring some of the risks associated with HRT.

Vaginal dryness

- use aqueous cream (available quite inexpensively from your pharmacist) instead of soap for the genital area
- see your doctor for advice about emollient creams if you suffer discomfort
- a variety of vaginal lubricants are on sale in pharmacies that can be used daily to lubricate the vagina and to ease intercourse when needed
- oestrogen is available on prescription specifically for use in this area. Creams and tablet pessaries can be inserted that will have an almost immediate effect on dryness and atrophy. These are not the same as HRT, having only a local effect, so they will not help with hot flushes.

Increased risk of osteoporosis (bone thinning)

- increase your bone density by taking exercise such as swimming, gardening, walking or golf
- eat a diet that includes plenty of calcium and vitamin D – green leafy vegetables, low fat dairy products, tinned fish
- get outdoors for at least 15 minutes every day to increase your production of vitamin D as this will help your body to process its calcium resources efficiently
- if you think you're at serious risk of osteoporosis (perhaps because of a family history), your doctor can check your situation and perhaps prescribe drugs.

Confusion and memory problems

- mental sharpness is a good example of the 'use it or lose it' remedy. Doing puzzles such as crosswords and Sudoku will help to keep those 'senior moments' at bay
- ballroom dancing can help. Not only is it a good exercise for everyone to take up but concentrating on and having to remember the steps also helps to keep the memory in good shape
- cut down on alcohol. Excessive alcohol consumption can speed up the brain's natural degenerative process and add to your concentration problems
- the alternative remedy 'Gingko Biloba' is believed to help with memory loss by improving blood flow to the brain.

General well-being

- there is plenty of evidence to suggest that including phytoestrogens in our diets can help us to cope with the menopause. Soya and linseeds are the richest sources but phytoestrogens are also found in cereals (oats, barley, couscous and bulgar wheat), seeds (sunflower, sesame, pumpkin, poppy), pulses (lentils, Soya beans), beans (chickpeas, kidney beans, haricot, broad beans) and vegetables (celery, peppers, garlic, onions, broccoli, tomatoes)
- stop smoking
- relax – take up yoga, have a massage, try reflexology or aromatherapy.

Hormone replacement therapy

There is no doubt that hormone replacement therapy (HRT) can help to relieve most women's menopausal symptoms. However, it comes with risks and side effects and should usually only be taken for a short time to get you through the difficult initial phase of the menopause. Whether or not you take HRT is a matter of personal choice but you should discuss your options with your GP before making your decision. He or she will be able to discuss the risks with you in detail. The main risk is that of breast cancer. This risk is greater the longer you take HRT and also increases if you take the combined hormone type of treatment. Oestrogen-only therapies have shown to be less risky but the risk is still there, so a full and frank discussion with your doctor is essential – especially if you have any other risk factors such as a family history of the disease.

If you are considering taking alternative therapies, you should also check these out with your doctor while you're discussing HRT. Your doctor will know whether these are appropriate for you and will be able to advise of any dangers associated with them, taking into account your medical history.

Alternative remedies

Black Cohosh is said to help with hot flushes and night sweats. It has not been extensively tested with regard to its effect on breast tissue so if this is a concern for you, speak with your doctor.

Red Clover Extract is a source of phytoestrogens that may help with general menopausal symptoms including hot flushes.

St John's Wort may help with stress caused by the menopause but consult your doctor before using this as it may react with a variety of prescribed drugs.

Wild Yam is a plant-based hormone substitute which may help with hot flushes.

Agnus Castus is recommended to help with mood swings. This – in tablet or tincture form – is prepared from berries and has a progesterone effect so should not be combined with progesterone drugs.

Dong Quai is a source of phytoestrogens. It is not recommended for diabetics.

Sage is available as tablets or as a tincture, which is more concentrated. Can be good for hot flushes and night sweats.

Soya Milk contains plant chemicals that mimic oestrogen. Just a small glass every day can be enough to make a difference.

Evening Primrose Oil may help with hot flushes.

Gingko Biloba can improve memory and general mental function.

Bach Flower remedies are a system of flower essences developed by a homeopathic doctor in the 1930s. Different ones can help with the menopause or symptoms such as stress or confusion.

In addition to these remedies, there are any number of branded tablets and potions that may contain a blend of these and other ingredients. Some of these are quite expensive, so some thought is required before opting for this sort of solution. You might want to try a few lifestyle changes before spending too much money.

> **Top tip**
>
> Remember that remedies do not work overnight. You will usually need to take them for a few weeks before you see any real benefit.

Breast cancer and other prevalent problems

Of all the cancers to which we are prone, breast cancer seems to be the one that women fear most. There are over 40,000 women diagnosed with breast cancer every year in the UK and the older you get, the higher your chances of getting it. The most important aspect of saving lives by cancer treatment is starting it as early as possible, so detection and prompt action is essential. All women over the age of 50 are entitled to a mammogram every three years as part of the national screening programme – it's important that you do the very best for yourself and take up the appointment. There are other ways in which you can help yourself including self-examination and following a healthy lifestyle.

Self-examination is easy and should be carried out regularly – perhaps once a month after your period or on the first day of each month if you're past the menopause or simply choose any day that you will find easy to remember so that you get into the habit of checking. The Breakthrough Breast Cancer charity advises that approximately 80% of breast cancers are found by women themselves, so checking your breasts every month could save your life. Follow these steps to check your breast for lumps and irregularities:

- Look at your breasts. Stand in front of a mirror and check your breasts' size, shape and position. Check for puckering or marking of the skin. Notice any changes in your nipples too.
- Now lie back and use your hand flat to feel both breasts in turn. With small, circular movements, you're feeling for any lumps or thickening – anything that feels different from usual. Make sure that you have covered the whole of your breast before you move on to the other one. It can help to imagine your breast divided into four sections and visit each section in turn to check.
- Check under your arm for lumps and bumps. Your lymph nodes are under your arms and this is where many irregularities show up.

- If you are in the least bit worried by anything you find, go immediately to your doctor. If it is nothing to worry about, your mind will be put at rest sooner, but if it is cancerous, then the sooner you start treatment the better your chances are of beating the disease.

Following a healthy lifestyle can reduce your risk of getting breast cancer. There is a lot of research going on to establish the exact nature of the risks of breast cancer. Many are concerned with the levels of oestrogen in our bodies (including drugs containing hormones e.g. HRT and the contraceptive pill) and other things such as our genes or when we have children – and these are very difficult for us to control – but maintaining a healthy lifestyle is thought to reduce our risk of developing breast cancer and also various other types of cancer or disease. The three main lifestyle changes we could make that may reduce our risk are:

- *Increasing levels of exercise* It is thought that incorporating exercise into your daily life can reduce the risk of cancer by up to 20 per cent.
- *Cutting alcohol consumption* Doctors are becoming increasingly worried about the binge drinking culture that is becoming prevalent among younger women. It seems sensible to ensure that our alcohol intake is kept within the recommended maximum levels (14 units per week for women).
- *Obesity* There is some evidence that, as fat produces a source of oestrogen, it can contribute to the risk of contracting breast cancer. Following a healthy diet and reducing weight if you are overweight is therefore a sensible precaution and will, of course, have lots of other benefits too.

If you do become one of the increasing number of women in their 50s who are diagnosed with breast cancer, there is now a much better chance that you will beat the disease and go on to live a long and healthy life. New treatments are continually being developed so there is no longer any need to think of a diagnosis of cancer as a death sentence. The treatment is rarely pleasant but lots of women have got through it and so can you. It may help to know a little about what the treatment involves. Each woman is treated according to the type of cancer and the stage of its development. Treatment may include:

- *Diagnosis* When you have been referred to the hospital by your doctor, you will usually have a series of tests to establish whether the lump is cancerous or not. This could include a mammogram (an X-ray where each breast is viewed from two sides while squashed between two plates on the machine), an ultrasound scan (a painless examination using a gel and an ultrasound machine), needle aspiration (removal of fluid from the affected area using a needle) or a tissue biopsy (removal of tissue from the lump). For these last two tests it may take a few days for laboratory results to become available.

- *Surgery* More and more women are having a lumpectomy (removal of just the cancerous lump and a margin of healthy tissue surrounding it) these days, instead of a complete mastectomy (removal of the entire breast). If a mastectomy is necessary – perhaps because the cancer has spread too far in the breast tissue or is particularly aggressive, reconstructive surgery is often available. During the operation the lymph nodes under the arm will also usually be removed for examination. Surgery for the removal of the cancer will often only require a day or two in hospital. When the results of the surgery – the removed tissue – are examined, the exact state of the cancer can be diagnosed and further treatment decided upon.

- *Chemotherapy* If the cancer has been found to have spread to the lymph nodes under the arm then chemotherapy is usually recommended. This is a harsh, drug-based treatment that can be given as an out-patient or an in-patient intravenously or in tablet form. This is what can cause the hair loss that is so feared by women who are diagnosed with breast cancer. It also causes nausea, stomach upsets, weight gain, fatigue, listlessness and a host of other side effects as it goes around the body killing cancer cells and, unfortunately, all sorts of other cells along the way.

- *Radiotherapy* This is localised radiation treatment to clear the area of any remaining cancerous cells. It can cause extreme fatigue, slight lung or throat damage and burned skin but is otherwise not painful or uncomfortable.

- *Drugs* After the main treatments are completed, women whose cancers have been found to be linked to the hormone oestrogen will usually be given inhibitors such as Tamoxifen or Arimidex. These are taken for five years (after that they have been shown to become ineffective) and can cause severe menopause-like symptoms such as hot flushes, night sweats, depression, loss of libido and vaginal dryness. They have been shown to reduce the risk of cancer returning by 50 per cent.

Famous – and not so famous – examples

There have been many celebrity cases of breast cancer reported over recent months and years – Kylie Minogue, Sheryl Crow, Marsha Hunt, Anastasia and Lynn Redgrave to name just a few – and each one of them will have been just as shocked and upset at their diagnosis as any of the 40,000-plus 'ordinary' women diagnosed in the UK last year. Three years ago I was one of those women. And I'm still here, writing this book and carrying on with my life almost as if it never happened. It has given me a new determination to get fit, to eat a healthy diet and to make the most of my life. The treatment and the after-effects are never pleasant but the most important thing to remember is that you can get through it. All of those celebrities have come out the other side and so have I. So, if you are given that awful news 'You have cancer', take your treatment and then get on with life in your 50s.

Incontinence

Another problem that often starts to affect women in their 50s is incontinence, which affects up to 20 per cent of the older female population. It affects women in particular for two reasons. First, you may have had trauma to the entrance to the bladder, the 'pelvic floor' or bowel during childbirth and second, during the menopause many women notice that their bladder becomes lax, with a leakage of urine. If you've noticed that you leak urine when you cough, laugh or move suddenly it's certainly worth talking to your doctor. It's not a normal part of growing older for women and you don't have to accept it. There are several things your doctor might suggest:

- pelvic floor exercises – these can strengthen your pelvic floor if you suffered damage during childbirth and will ensure less leakage of urine
- weight loss – excess weight can put pressure on your bladder
- treatment for anything that increases the pressure on the bladder, such as constipation or fibroids
- drug treatments – these can improve the muscle tone of the bladder

It is vital that you find help for this annoying problem and to persevere with the treatments. Left unchecked, incontinence can severely affect your quality of life as you get older.

Health issues for both sexes

Of course, not all the health problems that can affect your life in your 50s and beyond are restricted to women. There are many diseases and conditions that occur with ageing and affect both men and women such as:

- *Alzheimer's disease* Almost all cases of Alzheimer's occur in old age. It is a condition where memory and the ability to think clearly are gradually lost over time. Although there is no known way of preventing Alzheimer's there is some evidence to suggest that regular exercise, not being overweight, keeping cholesterol and blood pressure at normal levels, eating a healthy diet rich in antioxidants, vitamins C and E, and eating oily fish – in other words, keeping yourself as fit and healthy as you possibly can – may help to prevent it. Many health experts also recommend keeping your mind active by doing puzzles such as Sudoku or crosswords. It seems to be a case of 'use it or lose it' when it comes to memory and concentration.

- *Heart disease* Coronary heart disease (CHD) kills over four times more women than breast cancer does. Heart and circulatory disease is the number one killer of women, yet the myth persists that it is only overweight, middle-aged businessmen who suffer from CHD. Although women are less at risk in earlier life, after the menopause the risks are equal to men's. Research recommends cutting down on fatty foods, salt, alcohol and making sure you eat at least five portions of fruit and vegetables a day. You should also stop smoking, take exercise regularly and cut your stress levels. Although CHD is a big killer it is largely preventable and you should check your risk factors with your doctor and ask him or her to do some basic tests such as cholesterol levels and blood pressure.

- *Arthritis* There are two main types of this painful condition, both of which often show up as you reach mid-life. The first type, osteoarthritis, affects about a million people in the UK. Several factors seem to affect the likelihood of your getting the disease including being over 40, being female, and being overweight. The second type, rheumatoid arthritis, affects all ages but most commonly starts between 30 and 50. It affects approximately three times as many women as men. Again prevention is not yet an option but keeping fit and active can improve how you deal with the conditions if you get them.

- *Failing eyesight* A gradual falling off in sight used to be accepted as a normal part of ageing. This is true in some ways. For example, you'll be less able to focus on close objects as you get older. Also it's normal to need reading glasses as you reach 35 to 40, especially if you're long-sighted to start with. However, most people should continue to have good eyesight into their 80s or 90s. Cataracts affect older people – as many as 70% of people over 85 have them – but the advice must be the same as for any condition affecting the eyes. Consult an optician or your GP if you are concerned about your vision as your eyes are delicate and important.

Summary

In this chapter we have looked at some of the more difficult aspects of entering your 50s for women. These health issues, such as the menopause and breast cancer can, if not dealt with positively, result in problems that can drag down a woman's life. They can seriously affect her quality of life so a determined effort to deal with them and then get on with life is vital in mid-life. If, as is highly likely, you suffer from some – or, heaven forbid, all – of these symptoms and side effects, then you will need to develop some self-help strategies and a positive attitude towards your problems. We also looked at some of the other health issues that may occur at this time such as incontinence, arthritis and Alzheimer's disease and found that keeping fit and healthy in terms of weight and activity was our best defence against these problems. We also need to stay positive in order to cope well. Do this and look for help and you will not only get through this period but also come to see the multitude of opportunities offered by this decade without being too distracted by the health problems that it can also bring.

Action plan: helping yourself

The ten years from 50 to 60 can throw a lot of health issues at a woman but very few of them will turn out to be insurmountable problems. There will always be things that you can do to help yourself. Depending on the situation you're facing, you should now develop an action plan to help yourself:

- With the menopause, research your options. Check out HRT and other remedies with your GP. If you have a particular symptom, deal with it by trying one of the remedies suggested. Try it for a period of at least two months to let it get into your system and have a positive effect.

- Get into the habit of checking your breasts on a monthly basis and make a promise to yourself that you will not let fear stop you from consulting your doctor about any changes you find.
- Adapt your diet. Make sure that you are eating healthily – even if you do not need to lose weight. Cut down on salt and sugar and increase your intake of fruit and vegetables.

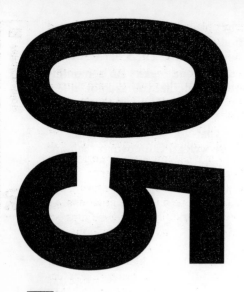

relationships

In this chapter you will learn:

- the importance of communication in your relationships
- how to deal with being alone
- how to overcome sex problems in middle age.

How we get on with the other people in our lives has a profound affect on our well-being. If we argue or have problems with the people around us – and by the time we get into our 50s there will be plenty of people in our lives: husbands, partners, sons and daughters, parents, friends, work colleagues to name just a few – then there will be obvious effects on our emotional state, but there will also be a noticeable affect on our physical state. Of course, well handled, our relationships can transform our lives and make them worth living, but badly handled they can make it a miserable existence. Our most important relationship – the one that will ultimately make the most difference to our lives – is that with our partner (if we have one) and entering our 50s can be a very difficult time. It can be a time of great change and involve physical, emotional and practical problems that we need to be able to cope with together. If, as is most common in our society, you are of a similar age to your partner then you will be both be going through these life changes together. Children leaving home, the menopause, physical changes, career problems, parents becoming dependent and so on can all take their toll on a relationship and divorce is becoming ever more common, so how can you 'damage-proof' your relationship? Well, making it totally immune to whatever life throws at it may be impossible but there are things to watch out for and a few 'rules' to follow that will make it less vulnerable.

Communication

It can't be said often enough – if you don't communicate, you're in trouble. And it's not just the amount of talking that you do that is important; the quality of that communication is relevant too. If your conversations are limited to what the children have done today or what your mother said, then you need to think again. There should be a bit of time in each day for you to catch up on each other's lives. This may be when one or both of you come home from work in the evening and collapse on the sofa with a cup of tea or a G&T. It may be during your evening meal. Or it may be last thing at night when the day is done and you can finally review it quietly together. Whenever is best for you is when you should make sure that you keep in touch with your partner's life and when they are allowed a peek into yours. Try not to make this a moaning session – there must have been some good bits to your day too! And if not, then discuss how you can make some good things happen. Talk about the changes that you can make in this decade of your lives. Talk about the holidays and weekends away that you can have – pleasing yourselves and developing your own interests now that the children have flown the nest. Above all, talk about your dreams and ambitions. As we've said before, you should still have some ambitions left at this stage in your life and you should feel secure enough to explore these fully with your partner.

Make an effort

Just because you've known and lived with this person for years and years doesn't mean that you can afford to ignore them. If you ignore them, they may just surprise you in a way that you won't like. So, show them your better side more often, talk to them with respect, show them affection, dress up (or at least get washed and changed out of your gardening gear) even if you're just staying in for the evening in front of the television with them, listen to them and try to understand their point of view and, above all, don't take them for granted.

If you can manage to put in a bit of extra effort on a daily basis, then your relationship will undoubtedly thrive. It is when a relationship has become comfortable and just routine that danger can be closest, so make an effort to live life to the full with your partner and then he or she may be around forever.

Tiny problems or everyday habits can become enormous irritations so it is important to make an effort to make allowances. If your partner has an annoying little habit try not to make a big deal of it – you probably have your own little habits that would try anyone's patience. A little understanding and a lot of respect will go a long way.

Communication exercise

If you find it difficult to talk to your partner, or feel that he or she never listens, try this exercise:

The idea is to take time to communicate. Take turns to talk to or listen to your partner without interruption. To make it work you need to set time aside and follow the guidelines.

1 Toss a coin to decide who will talk first. The other listens without interruption until ten minutes are up and then they take a turn at talking.

2 Talk about anything that comes into your head but try not to make it an excuse to 'have a go'. If you run out of things to talk about, don't worry. Just use your time to consider what you have already said and why you don't have more to say. It can be useful to try starting all your sentences with 'I'. This way you should get to talking about your feelings and desires.

3 Listen without interrupting. Just nod or signal that you're listening in some non-verbal way. Say nothing until it's your turn. Then try not to respond to what your partner has just said. This is your opportunity to talk about your opinions and feelings – create your own agenda, don't follow theirs.

4 When the session is up, do not talk about what's been said until at least the following day. Give yourselves time to think about what's been said and for feelings to cool if you really disagree.

The act of talking while knowing that you are not going to be interrupted can be very liberating and will allow you and your partner to air your thoughts and opinions. It might be that you find it so useful that you decide to do this little exercise on a regular basis.

Getting older together

If you've been together for some time, you have probably developed a way of living with each other that involves tolerance, a sense of humour and lots of love. As you grow older, this will not change – you will still need to make allowances and to work at your relationship. As you approach retirement you will need to be sure that the way of life that has developed is acceptable to you both. Are you both happy with your life, contented with one another's company and ready to welcome a bit more time together? Or will you find it intolerable to spend more time together? Have you thought about how you will both be spending your time? This is something that you need to do together. There is little point in one of you happily contemplating a retirement out and about, seeing friends every day and pursuing various hobbies while the other is looking forward to spending time at home together. If you find yourself with wildly varying dreams of life when you're older, plenty of compromise will be called for. It is vital that you are able to reach a balance in your lives that will suit you both.

Here's where effort and understanding will come in again. How we deal with our partner will always have an effect on our happiness. Life can be immeasurably improved by a good relationship or destroyed by a bad one, so it is obviously in your interest to nurture the closeness you have with your partner. As you head through your 50s towards retirement or at least a lessening of work responsibilities, this is especially important. You will have the capacity to make your partner's life happier and less stressful in the years to come and they have the same influence over your life. You will, of course, have to build your own life and develop your own interests to keep you happy in the decades to come and your partner will have to do the same, but communication, understanding and goodwill along the way will make life far easier.

Being alone – enjoy it or change it

Many single, middle-aged people are perfectly happy with their own company and dread having someone else around on a permanent basis that might upset their routines. There are others who are married or in a live-in relationship but wish they weren't, so it's obvious that living as a couple is not the perfect solution for everyone. But other single people are far from happy alone and dread the thought of being alone forever. It is these people – the ones who are not 'single and happy to be so' – that this section addresses.

The first piece of advice is, initially, not to look too hard for a partner. There are two reasons for this. First, being on your own after a bereavement or when a relationship has broken up can be difficult to get used to but when you have given it some time you may come to realise that you're enjoying yourself. In any event, you need to give yourself some time to get over a broken relationship. Second, being too eager to find a new live-in partner can be scary to some potential partners. No matter how hard you try to hide your desire for commitment, it will show. Far better to develop a social life that involves your meeting a variety of people of both sexes. Try to get out and about a couple of times a week, no matter how much you feel you just want to hide away from all the people who seem to be part of a happy couple or who might be looking at you with pity. Look for hobbies, societies or sports in which you can take part in and perhaps learn something along the way and, while you're busy enjoying yourself, you will be meeting people who might just include a potential new partner.

Where to meet new people

There are lots of places and situations where you will be able to increase your social circle and enrich your life. You could try:

- getting out and about with existing friends and taking a real interest in people to whom you are introduced
- evening classes. This is not just the old cliché. If you go to a class that might appeal to a variety of people, you will come into contact with new people – not just men with a view to dating them – and will, with the right attitude and a bit of confidence be able to find things you have in common with them which you can develop into a social contact
- volunteer work. While you're working and doing some good, you might be pleasantly surprised by just how many contacts you can make
- any club or organization that catches your interest. Perhaps you would like to help to save the environment or to help organize events in your town – whatever it is, you will come into contact with people who are on your wavelength
- sports clubs. If you fancy a go at badminton, yoga or tennis, for example, you will be able to socialize with the other people who take part
- personal columns in local and national newspapers – but take note of the precautions you should take as detailed in the Internet dating section later in this chapter. You can meet both female and male companions or partners in this way
- dinner clubs. This is where you can attend a meal in local restaurants with other members of the club. Find out what is available in your area, gather up your courage and join in.

When you have come to terms with your single state and have built up a healthy social life, you might start to contemplate going on a date or two. If you had been with your previous partner for some years and are maybe not as confident about your looks as you used to be, this can be a difficult time. The answer is to take it slowly and try to put the following advice into action:

- View the date as just a night out with a friend and resolve to enjoy yourself.
- Try to get the person you're with to talk about themselves – it's flattering for someone to take an interest in you and everyone can talk about themselves.

- Try not to worry about what you look like. Your date will be just as worried about what you think of them and it is likely that (unless your date is 20 or 30 years younger than you!) they will be feeling their age too and will be worrying about their wrinkles or their fat tummy or thick ankles...
- Don't think that sex is compulsory early in a relationship. Sex is for when both of you feel like it so don't feel pressurized or worried.
- Think of a couple of questions to get the conversation started. Nothing too nosy – perhaps 'what sort of music do you like?' or 'do you like sports?' Once you've got the conversation under way it will start to flow but don't feel that it's all down to you. Give your friend space to ask questions and don't be afraid of gaps in the conversation.
- Make sure you don't spend the entire evening talking about your previous relationship. Whether it was so good that you miss it or so bad that you can't understand how you ever got into it, it will not make a good topic of conversation for a first date and brief details should be saved for later.
- Stay optimistic no matter how the date turns out. Your new life is only just beginning and, at your age, it has plenty of promise.

Many newly single people in their 50s have great fun with Internet dating. There are agencies for all types of people. It's the twenty-first-century equivalent of the personal columns in newspapers but is much more fun and, in some ways, safer. Despite what we all hear about chat rooms being dangerous, this usually refers to defenceless youngsters, not to mature, clued-up women. There are obvious precautions you must take until you've learned a bit about the chat rooms and the people who are in them:

- Don't give out too much personal information – such as your telephone number or address.
- Take it slowly. If someone is interested in you and you are interested in them, it is perfectly possible to develop a relationship that will build over time until it becomes desirable for you to meet. You will know when you have reached this stage and have learned enough about someone.
- Look for clues that suggest when someone is not telling the whole truth. Married people may be pretending they are single and many people will understate – or sometimes even overstate – their age. If something does not feel quite right, take care.

- Meet in a neutral place. If you've built up a rapport online then you will no doubt recognize one another when you meet by the Town Hall or outside a bar.
- Don't be desperate. A relationship with just anyone is definitely not better than no relationship at all, so wait for the right one to come along and develop.
- Be aware of possible problems. Gambling or drinking addictions and severe money problems are a no-no as is, of course, a wife or long-term partner still in the background and great differences in religious beliefs. But be tolerant – at least until you've found out a bit more. If your prospective partner is of a similar age to you, then they will have baggage. There may be children and other commitments and there will almost certainly have been other partners in the past but none of these are a bar to a good relationship.
- Enjoy yourself – that's why you're here.

Sex in your 50s

Sex in your 50s can be better than ever – the fear of pregnancy has gone, maybe the children have left home and you have some privacy at last and you may be with a well-loved and familiar partner who understands what you want. But there are lots of things that can cause problems at this time. These can be either caused by the physical effects of ageing or by changes within the relationship.

Both men and women can experience physical changes that affect their ability or desire to have sex. The menopause in women can have various symptoms such as vaginal dryness, sleepless nights caused by hot sweats, depression and a loss of libido that will disrupt – if not finish altogether – what was previously an enjoyable sex life. Meanwhile men may be experiencing erection problems or loss of libido caused by illnesses such as diabetes or prostrate problems. The way to get through these problems in a long-term relationship is by talking and understanding. If you are a woman plagued by the menopause then you must make sure that your partner knows what you are going through. With understanding, it should be possible to get through a difficult time and resume your sex life along previous lines. There are lots of things that women can try to overcome the problems caused by vaginal dryness and they should certainly seek help if it is affecting their love life. The same advice applies to men experiencing erection problems – get some help and talk about it with your partner. It is essential in both cases that partners understand that it is a physical problem and does not mean a lack of sexual attraction to them. Going off sex does not necessarily mean that you have gone off your partner.

Relationship changes

Relationship problems may be even more difficult to overcome. For many people the 50s are a time when we take stock and reassess our lives. We enter a new phase of our lives when children leave home, for example, or have a confidence crisis about our age and suddenly notice this person we may have been living with for many years and think that we don't really know them or even that we don't really like them. They may realise that the two young people they used to be have disappeared while they were busy raising a family or forging their way in careers and it becomes obvious that the whole relationship needs a makeover. If the relationship feels boring or too routine it is probable that the sexual relationship will have deteriorated. If you want to revitalize your relationship it is best to start with your daily lives and the following may help with this:

- Try re-discovering what you used to do together. If, before your family came along and became your priority, you used to go to pop concerts together, for example, decide on an artist you both like and go along to their next gig in your area. Or try dancing or cycling if you used to enjoy it when you were younger. Having shared interests is one of the things that will keep you together in old age as well as keeping you active and healthy.
- Talk. Really talk. It may be that you usually talk about the children and their problems or what happened at work and have not really talked to one another as friends for many years. This period of re-evaluation can be the perfect time to discover things about your partner and about yourself. Find out what you both really want out of life. Discuss your likes and dislikes (nothing is outside the scope of this – get to know your partner's favourite music, sports, foods, TV programmes and anything else you can think of) what dreams and hopes you have for the future and what you have already accomplished and feel proud of.
- Show consideration at all times. The person you live with is entitled to your respect and care and you should not forget that they have their own life to lead.

By reviving the relationship with your partner and understanding who they really are, it may be possible to revive or revitalise your sex life. When consideration and friendship are neglected in a relationship it is often the case that sex becomes undesirable, so the reverse can be true. The most important aspect of any relationship is communication, so talk honestly about your concerns and together you will be able to improve the situation.

Some high-profile examples

If you are in any doubt that a fulfilling sex life can carry on into mid-life and later life, just consider some high profile, sexy-looking women who marry again and again. Take Elizabeth Taylor and Joan Collins: they seem to fall in love – and in lust – repeatedly. What they have in common is an attitude to life that says, 'Bring it on, I want more' and they get more. Often the husbands of women like this are much younger than they are but they appear to be satisfied by their seriously attractive, forward-looking wives.

Summary

Relationships can transform our lives – they can make us supremely happy or contented or they can make us miserable – so it is important to get them sorted out. As we enter different stages of our lives, there will be different problems that come along and which have to be dealt with. In all cases, communication with the people around us and making an effort to appreciate them and their point of view will pay dividends.

If we're looking for a relationship, then it is important that we take great care and take things slowly.

Sex problems sometimes come along when we are in our 50s and there can be two general reasons for this. One is that the changes caused by ageing or illness will result in physical problems that make sex difficult and it is vital in this case to remember that we should be looking for a solution to the physical problems rather than worrying about how our partners feel about us; i.e. don't take it personally. The other common reason for sex problems is that there are underlying difficulties in the relationship, possibly caused by changes that often happen in our lives at this time. In this case it may be necessary to revitalise the relationship by getting to know each other better as we enter this different stage in our lives.

Action plan: staying happy

Whether you are in a long-term relationship or not, you undoubtedly have plenty to be grateful for. Some days it might not seem like that but the trick to staying happy is to be aware of all that is right with your world. Some people are experts at seeing the bright side of everything while others always see the negatives in a situation. This action plan involves being satisfied with the relationship aspect of your life.

If you have a partner, resolve to find three things every day about him or her and about your life together that you appreciate. Just three things every day that make you happy. These could be anything from their bringing you an early morning cup of tea in bed to being grateful for their financial contribution to your life or the affection they show you.

If you are not currently in a relationship and are living alone you will need to find three things every day that you appreciate about your single life. It might be that you particularly relish being able to watch just what you like on the television without having to think about anyone else's likes and dislikes or you are grateful for your complete independence.

The point of this action plan is to count your blessings. By doing this on a regular basis you will be helping yourself to stay happy.

06

younger generations

In this chapter you will learn:
- some tips on dealing with your offspring
- the advantages of having children in mid-life
- how to enjoy your grandchildren.

Dealing with younger people can be both rewarding and problematical. When your children have grown up and you are finally able to establish a relationship with them that does not involve their complete dependence upon you, the closeness and affinity that you have with them as adults can be extremely satisfying. If, however, your offspring are now adults but are still living at home with you, it can sometimes be difficult not to feel some resentment when the old arguments from their teenage years continue and you seem to have to battle with them simply to be able to live your own life. Some offspring still living at home have difficulty in making the adjustment to adults and truly believe that they still deserve to be the centre of attention – just as they were when they were children. For the sake of your own sanity, you must disabuse them of this notion. Make them see that they have options – they could buy or rent their own home where they would be in charge and be able to set all the rules, or they could remain in your home where you are in charge and things are run according to your requirements rather than theirs. With today's property prices, some young people are in a position where they are unable to afford to move out into a home of their own. If this is the case with your children, then maybe a solution to both their problem and yours is for you to come to some arrangement whereby you could invest in a property jointly with your son or daughter.

Of course, your children will probably not be the only young people with whom you come into contact. If you had your children relatively young, then you may now be faced with another generation of young people – your grandchildren. There's more about enjoying your grandchildren later in this chapter.

They're not children any more

If your offspring are of an age to work and support themselves – and this applies to university students too, even though they may not be working and you may still be supporting them financially – then they are no longer children. In this case, you will need to stop treating them like helpless infants. If they have left home but keep coming back every time they have a tiny problem (usually involving their inefficient control of their finances!) then you will need to set some limits. Make it clear that your money and your time is just that – yours. You and they will both have to come to terms with the fact that sometimes, when they ask for a favour, you will have to say 'no'. If you are in the habit of always helping out your hapless offspring, this may seem harsh and difficult at first, but you must remember the old adage that 'you have to be cruel to be kind'. Your aim as a parent should be to ensure your children are equipped to deal with the world as it is and this involves supporting themselves and running their own lives. Try saying 'no' once in a while to their request for a loan or babysitting at short notice or ironing a bagful of shirts. Very few – if any – of their requests will be life-threatening or even very important and the sooner they realise that their lives are their own responsibility, the better it will be for everyone involved.

Having children in mid-life

The average age at which women have children has risen in the last decade or two. This is partly because of the technological advances that have fuelled improvements in fertility treatment, allowing women who had given up hope of getting pregnant chances of having a family. It is also because of the changes that have gone on in women's lives. Many women nowadays choose to develop their careers before they start a family or they remarry in their 30s or 40s and decide to have a family with their new partners. Both of these changes have resulted in women continuing to become pregnant in their late 30s, 40s or even into their 50s. The growing trend for second marriages has also resulted in many older women looking after children as they take on the children of their new, perhaps younger partner.

All these changes mean that many women find themselves looking after children in mid-life and find that there are advantages and disadvantages of late motherhood. The disadvantages include:

- higher risks during pregnancy. Problems such as Down's syndrome become more likely in an older mother. At 35 the risk is 1 in 400 but at over 45 the risk increases to 1 in 32. Miscarriage is also more common in women over 35 and problems such as high blood pressure or pregnancy-induced diabetes are also more common
- tiredness during pregnancy. It is important to rest as much as possible during pregnancy and it may also be necessary to start maternity leave earlier if you are an older mother-to-be.

Despite the disadvantages, most mature mothers-to-be would say that they would prefer being older than being a very young new mother. The negative feelings many people have about older mothers-to-be probably date back to several decades ago when the health problems were not easy to overcome and women were far less healthy in general. Now, most problems can be dealt with and women – whatever their age – start pregnancy in far better condition than in their grandmothers' days. The advantages include:

- a happy mother. Having followed a career or travelled or invested in property and done all the things she wanted to do before motherhood, a more mature mother-to-be will be ready to settle down and look after a child
- older mothers are more likely to breastfeed
- a confident mother. Maturity brings with it experience and this leads to an ease that transfers itself to the baby. A confident mother will also handle the inevitable decision-making much more easily
- increased likelihood of a family network to help out with childcare. A woman who has a baby in her 20s is likely to have a mother who is in her 40s or 50s whereas a woman having a baby in her 40s will probably have a mother who is old enough to be retired. The grandmother of the new baby is therefore more likely to be willing and available to baby-sit
- a more settled income. If the mother-to-be has been developing her career, the income available to support the baby is likely to be greater and more secure, making life easier in lots of ways. Financial security is always a plus point for a new family
- an established relationship. Many very young mothers start their families when their relationship with the father is in its very early days and they will often be learning to be a wife or partner at the same time as they are learning to be a mother. Older mothers will often be in a well-established relationship and consequently have fewer worries.

As you can see, there are lots of advantages to having children in later life and it is a far from impossible or unpleasant way to spend your 40s and 50s. It is not necessary to be some sort of superwoman to bring up a child in later life; what you lack in energy you will make up for in experience. If it is something that you really want to do then the right attitude – a positive, can-do, determined and compassionate attitude – will make it work and regardless of your age, things will be OK.

Enjoying your grandchildren

When I asked a group of friends – all mothers over 50 – what was the main advantage of turning 50, the unanimous answer was 'grandchildren'. They all felt that the joy and rewards that relationships with their grandchildren brought were well worth the extra wrinkles, the weight around the middle and the creaky joints that their 50s had also brought. The same would apply to those of us who have not had children of our own, but have played active roles in the lives of our nieces and nephews or God children and are now beginning to enjoy a new generation.

Grannies these days (and anyone else in this age group – aunties, Godmothers and so on) are far from the traditional view of a little grey-haired old lady sitting in a rocking chair, knitting. A twenty-first-century grandmother is far more likely to be a glamorous career woman with highlighted hair and an appointment to get her nails done. Despite the other things going on in their lives, grandparenthood is obviously still popular among 50-somethings and one of the attractions is probably the close relationship with a child unaccompanied by the constant pressure that is usually the fate of parents. A relationship with a grandchild can be fun and a chance to re-experience all the things you enjoyed when your own children were little – the trips out, the toys, the pride and the fun of buying new baby clothes to name just a few of the delights that await new grandparents.

The fun of a grandchild is there to be enjoyed, but some grandmothers do find it difficult for a number of practical reasons. Quite often a woman in her 50s will find herself with grandchildren but also with a career and she may not be able to spend as much time as she would like with them. In this situation, it is important to slow down a little and make some time to see – and enjoy – the new addition to the family. Just as with your own children's childhoods, time passes far too quickly, and by the time you have got through that busy period at work, the opportunity to spend time with the toddler who loves his granny may well have passed. And that will leave you with nothing but regrets. Another reason that today's grandparents may find it difficult to spend time with their grandchildren is that many of us now live long distances from our offspring and the daily 'pop-in' visits that were a feature of our grandparents' lives, will have become impossible. In this case, different arrangements will have to be made to compensate. Perhaps weekend stopovers can take the place of the shorter visits and this would satisfy both the grandparents who will get to know their grandchildren and the parents who will get some time to themselves.

Of course, amid all these joys of grandparenthood, there are also problems. One that often arises is the feeling of being over-used and under-valued. If you are asked to help out with childcare, it is important to make clear that you have commitments and a life of your own. Set out when you are available and will be happy to help and try not to be persuaded into taking on responsibility for the care of your grandchildren when you would rather be doing something else. Of course, life is not always as simple as this. It might be that your children cannot afford childcare and have turned to you when they are desperate for help. Remember that you can still say 'no'. Be sure that the parents are not overstating their financial problems. Do they both really need to work or could one of them stay at home with your grandchildren if they cut back on some of the things that they spend their money on? Have they really researched all possibilities of childcare in their area? Could one of them work part time? Could they juggle their working hours so that they can manage childcare between them? All parents are now entitled to ask to work flexibly, i.e. to change their working hours to suit family responsibilities. Could they start and finish early so that they could collect their children from school and you could maybe juggle your commitments to be able to do the school run in the mornings. Try to think of all the possible solutions to the problem rather than simply making your own life difficult to make your child's life easier.

Another thorny issue is that of advice – often seen by new parents as interference. Try not to ring several times a day and also to remember that things have certainly changed since you were bringing up your children. The advice currently being given out to new mothers on things such as first aid and whether to lay a child to sleep on their tummies or on their backs is different to that given out 30 or so years ago. If your grandchildren are being fed on demand then that is just how it is, so there is little point in your disapproving or repeatedly stating that when your son was young he only got fed every four hours. Try to think back to how you felt when you had your babies. You wanted to raise your child your way, didn't you? So, summon up all your powers of understanding and leave the new parents to do just that. Your job is to be there as much as you can when they need help in the early stages and to remember just how exhausting it can all be.

The practicalities of looking after babies and young children may well come as a shock – all over again – when you first become a grandmother, so try these few rules and tips to make life a bit easier:

- Don't give advice unless you're asked for it.
- Get used to all the equipment. You probably didn't have one of these fancy buggies when you had your children – or maybe a baby-listening device or maybe even the disposable nappies, so make sure that you can use all the equipment. Practice folding and unfolding the buggy and make sure that you understand how the other things work and when you will use them.
- Keep some treats – sweets, chocolate buttons or dried fruit – ready to use as bribes or just as treats. But make sure that what you give the little ones would meet with the parents' approval and that you're ready to clear up the mess afterwards.
- Make sure you've got a supply of tissues and wet wipes ready to mop up chocolaty faces, runny noses and dirty hands and knees.
- Keep in touch on a regular basis. Try not to ring so often as to be a nuisance but to ring often enough that you know what is going on in your grandchildren's lives. You could also drop them funny little cards in the post or email or text them as they get older.
- Put yourself in charge of the photo albums. Keep a record of all the important stages of your grandchildren's lives and keep the snaps organised in albums – they may well become family heirlooms.

Another way in which you might want to treat your grandchildren is by looking after their future financially. If you've reached a stage in your life where you have pretty much everything you want and have looked after your own financial future via savings and pensions, you can make investments on your grandchildren's behalf. There are, as ever, tax considerations and limits as to how much you can invest for each grandchildren in any tax year so you should take expert advice on this. There are specialist savings plans that are particularly suited to this sort of long-term investment (you probably won't want the money to become available to your grandchildren until they are going to university or starting out in life) or, if your grandchildren are about to go to university, a property investment might be appropriate so that your grandchild will have somewhere decent to live – rent free – and you will have your investment intact so that you could still sell and give a proportion to your grandchild. There are lots of options available, as with any investment, and it is worth giving it a lot of thought and then getting expert advice.

The most important thing about having grandchildren is to enjoy them. You may have to make allowances for some things that will be different in this new generation and the next section will give you a bit more detail about this.

Understanding young people

If you feel that your children had a different upbringing to you, then the society into which your grandchildren are being introduced will bear almost no resemblance to how the world was when you were their age. Given the different rules and surroundings, it is little wonder that they have ways of doing things or behaviour that is in such stark contrast to us. Take a moment to think of all the things that your grandchildren take for granted but which you would never even have dreamed of when you were young – computers, colour televisions, perhaps your mother going out to work, going to school in a car, material possessions that may, at times, seem excessive (but a good grandparent won't say so too loudly), a shower every day (didn't you have a bath just once or twice a week?), computer games, mobile phones, ten-year-old girls in make-up, flying abroad every year (but then, have they been on a train or a bus? If not, that might be looked on as a treat that granny can arrange) and everyone in the family expecting to go to university. Now think of the changes that have happened in society during your lifetime that your grandchildren will have accepted as normal – violence on television, sex education, political correctness, equality for women, no corporal punishment in schools, asylum seekers, shops open on Sundays, a decline in church and Sunday school attendance, almost all families possessing a car and a rise in living standards. All of these things make up a completely different world to the one you were living in when you were young. The last 40 years or so have seen tremendous change in both material things and in the values of society. Different levels of behaviour in all sorts of areas are now the norm and it is these that your grandchildren will be complying with. They will not be expected in their daily lives to 'speak only when spoken to' or to 'make do and mend'. Rather they will have their own points of view on most subjects and will expect to be able to express them and will expect to maintain the standards of material possessions which they have become used to. For these reasons you will have to modify your behaviour when dealing with the young people brought up in today's society. You will not be able to impose your standards or values but must accept those that have already been passed on – from their parents and from the world in which they live – and deal with the reality.

So, while you can bring your wide experience to your relationships with young people, you must remember that they also have experiences that are just as valid as yours and will affect their point of view.

Summary

There is no doubt that life has changed beyond recognition in the last few decades. Modern technology, political developments, changes in society – especially those involving the position of women in society – have all contributed to the vast changes that have taken place. In making the most of our relationships with younger people when we are in our 50s, we must remember that they have different experiences and that these will give them a different point of view. These different points of view are just as valid as our own and we must make allowances for them. We must not assume that we are always right and that we know better than our offspring or our grandchildren as this is a sure-fire way of spoiling relationships with them. In exactly the same way as in our relationships with our contemporaries, mutual respect and plenty of patience and understanding will result in more rewarding relationships with the young people in our lives.

Action plan: improving your relationships with the young people in your life

How you deal with the young people in your life will depend, to a large extent on the age of those young people. Babies and toddlers can be enjoyed at face value. You will, of course, have to take into account their parents' preferences regarding standards of behaviour, punishments, treats and so on, but it will mostly be simply a case of enjoying their company.

Older children and teenagers are a different matter. As we discussed earlier in this chapter, they will often have their own opinions and will expect to be able to express them. Understanding the differences between their world and yours will help to make the relationship easier and who better to ask about these differences than the young people themselves? You may end up having some extremely interesting conversations. Here are a number of questions you could consider asking:

- What do you think life was like when I was a little girl?
- What sorts of punishments are there if people misbehave at school?
- What sort of behaviour from adults do you think is not acceptable?
- What sort of behaviour from people of your age do you think is not acceptable?
- What do you think it was like for women before equality?

Make sure that you let them talk when they want to and only give your point of view when you feel they are genuinely interested in it or when the conversation is drying up. If you can get this sort of conversation going, you will be sure to understand young people better at the end of it.

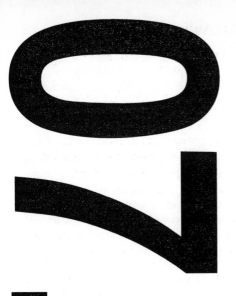

07

parents

In this chapter you will learn:
- how to manage your relationships with the older generation
- about the decisions you may have to make involving your parents
- how to prepare for the next decade.

If you're in your 50s, then your parents, if they are still alive, will be in their 70s or older and may now be needing some help with their day-to-day care. Most of us don't give a thought to the problems of caring for old people until it suddenly becomes a necessity. When it becomes obvious that your mother or father (or maybe it's your aunt or uncle or some other relative) is no longer able to look after themselves properly, feelings of panic may be induced. The decisions that are made at this point are important because they may have far-reaching effects for all the people concerned – you as the carer as well as the old person needing care and anyone else involved. You will need to take into account a variety of things in making the decision about future care and you may find that it is far from straightforward. Obviously, a spur of the moment decision is inadvisable and, if at all possible, some research should be done well in advance. Your decision as to what you must do will probably be based around three possible scenarios:

- the old person remains in their own home and you (and possibly other relatives) will visit to provide regular care
- the old person remains in their own home and you pay for someone to come in on a daily basis to provide care
- the old person takes up residence in a care home that will be responsible for their personal care.

There are pros and cons for all of these options and, rather than being a free decision weighing up the various factors, it is more likely to be a decision where the only solution quickly comes to the fore. It may be that the old person refuses to leave their home and has savings that they wish to make available to cover their care. Or one or more relatives may be insisting on helping the old person to retain some independence and are willing and able to help with daily care. Or it may be that the relative is completely incapable of remaining in their home and then the question will move on to the type of care homes that are available.

Managing your relationships with the older generation

Just as your children and grandchildren have lived a life that is very different to yours, with a different world as a backdrop, so your parents' generation will have a distinct set of experiences that will have formed their values and attitudes. It is likely that they spent at least a few years of their lives in the midst of a world war. Imagine how that would colour your view of the world. They would have been in some frightening situations with perhaps only the radio or newspapers for news about exactly what was going on (rather than the 24-hour blanket coverage that we have now), they may have been evacuated and had to live with a set of strangers and they will certainly have experienced a totally different diet to yours because of rationing. When you moan about the lack of some foodstuff or other that you have forgotten to buy, consider how ungrateful and spoiled that must make you seem to them. They have seen all the changes in society that you have plus plenty more.

Making allowances for these differences will certainly help your relationship along. You may also have to allow for their physical and mental state. They may have become unable to get around like they used to or their mental faculties may have become impaired. By the time your parents have become old people, your relationship will have evolved and become settled and it will probably be difficult to force any changes on it, so careful handling of any changes in their lives will be necessary. If you have always been treated as a child in the relationship, with them frequently advising and helping you, you will not be able to suddenly become the person in charge. However, it is far better to try to be prepared for the inevitable changes than to wait until an awkward situation becomes an emergency. If you know that your mother or father is becoming increasingly frail and will eventually have to have help with personal care then it would probably be easier for them to accept small changes such as help with shopping or with the bigger jobs such as window cleaning or lawn mowing long before the need becomes too great and you are having to force help for more personal care on them. Then, when the time comes to engage some help in the more personal tasks such as washing and dressing, they may find it easier to accept. Of course, some old people are fiercely independent and will never willingly accept help with such things and in this case it may be necessary to enlist the help of an outsider – someone from Social Services for example, to push through the necessary changes. Make sure you know what your parent's wishes are and have discussed all the possible solutions with them – even if they don't want to listen or you think they don't understand – and also that you do not accept any more work or responsibility than you can reasonably cope with. The shift from being the carer to becoming the cared-for will not be easy for independent people, but with care, respect and tact – plus a little resourcefulness – it can be managed to everyone's advantage and satisfaction.

Making decisions

Many decisions will have to be made as your parents get older and become less able to manage their affairs. However, it should not be assumed that you, as the offspring or carer, should make them all. The only time when you should have to make a decision alone is if either of your parents is in danger or severe distress and is completely unable to sort themselves out. Until or unless that scenario occurs, you should always assume that your parent (or elderly relative) will play a part in deciding what will happen to them. Decisions will have to be arrived at as to things such as the care arrangements to be made, how those arrangements will be paid for, whether your parent's property may have to be sold, how much help they need, what adaptations to their surroundings might make things easier for them, who will provide the care required and, if relevant, which care home your parent should be going into. There might even be decisions as to what treatment in hospital your parent will be prepared to accept.

Most – if not all – of the necessary decisions will, as we have already said, have to be made in consultation with your relative and keeping them involved in the process should be your first priority – even if you do not think that they are able to understand everything that is going on. You may also find it useful, or even essential, to involve professionals in the decision-making. A social worker, benefits advisor or representative of a care home will usually be able to provide the information that you all need to be able to reach a decision. It is always essential, though, to do your own research. There are books available on care arrangements and there are lots of leaflets that can be obtained from organisations such as Age Concern or from Citizens Advice Bureaux as well as the wealth of information that is provided by Social Services and the Department of Work and Pensions (see back of this book for details of how to get in touch with these organisations). During your research you should check out what benefit payments you are likely to be eligible for. For example, the elderly person may be entitled to an attendance allowance or you, as a carer, may be able to get a carer's allowance. After you've checked out the situation, you will probably need to have a full care assessment. You are entitled to request one of these where a social worker will visit the elderly person, see what they can and can't do and then make a decision on what care is needed and what help can be given.

Don't take a guilt trip

Whatever you do about the arrangements for your parents' future care, do not be railroaded into committing yourself to something that you find unacceptable. It is easy and very common to feel guilty about organising for someone outside your family to provide some personal care for your parents or elderly relative or for making arrangements for them to go into a care home. But feeling guilty is not a good reason for taking on responsibility for the physical care of a parent or anyone else you love. Being a carer is an extremely difficult and time-consuming role and not everyone is suitable for it or even capable of it. If you take on these onerous duties simply because you feel guilty, there is every likelihood that you will end up resenting the person you are looking after and making your own life miserable. It is quite likely too, that you will not be making the most appropriate arrangements for your relative. Any help you commit yourself to should be freely given, offered willingly and it should also fit into your life while leaving you time to live your own life. Consider all the practicalities of the situation and be realistic about what you can cope with, both physically and emotionally.

Summary

In this chapter we have looked at the issues that face you as your parents grow older and less able to look after themselves. The three most important points are:

- to make sure that you consult with your parents or elderly relatives regarding what their wishes are
- not to commit yourself to something with which you can't cope
- to do adequate research about all the options available to you.

Action plan: preparing for the next decade

Make a review now of your parents' situation (and, of course, of any other elderly relative or person for whom you may have to take some responsibility). Include the following:

- *Their wishes* Find out, well before they become incapacitated, what their expectations are regarding care they may need in later years, their attitude to care homes and to having people in their homes to help out with personal care.

- *Their finances* This may be a difficult subject for some people, especially the older generation who may not be accustomed to being as open about their financial arrangements as their offspring have learned to be. The money – or lack of it – that is set aside for ensuring a comfortable old age will have a major impact on what can be provided and what you may have to contribute. If your parents or relatives are still in a situation where they can do something about their financial situation before the problems of old age take over, then now is the time to think about what needs to be done.

- *Their will* If they haven't made one make sure that they do so. A properly made out and witnessed will can save untold problems later.

- *Who will have responsibility?* Will the whole responsibility for your parents fall on your shoulders or do you have siblings who will be able to share the cost and the effort?

- *Any specific health problems* If they have already suffered a heart attack, are diabetic or disabled in some way then now is the time to get prepared for the additional problems these issues may bring in old age.

- *Their property* Is it suitable for older people? Will it need any adaptation to help them to carry on living there after they become less agile or able? Is it too big for one or two pensioners now? Is the garden manageable? Alterations such as paving over the lawn or fitting a chair lift on the stairs now could save a lot of effort and expense when they become essential later. If there is something that you and they can do to make life easier, then it may be better to do it now while your parents can still have a say in the matter.

- *Their location* Think carefully about a change of location in old age. You will need to weigh up the benefits and the drawbacks very carefully. The advantage of being closer to members of the family who will be able to help out on a daily basis may be outweighed by the social isolation an older person may feel when faced with unfamiliar locations or a lack of shops and local facilities to which they can walk – however slowly.

If you have a comprehensive look at your parents' situation now and try to predict what will affect it in the future, it may prove beneficial all round. Forward planning may make you all feel more optimistic and reassured that any problems can be overcome and the fear of the unknown will not be given a chance of getting hold.

08

your home

In this chapter you will learn:
- how to make the most of an empty nest
- what to consider when downsizing
- how to decide if buying a property abroad is right for you.

Lots of changes go on in your mid-life and many of them affect where you live. You may need less space because of the children leaving home or you may need more space if you are planning to look after an elderly relative in your home. You may be worried about maintenance and finances as you approach retirement and decide to downsize for these reasons. Alternatively, you may be thinking of retiring to the sun or making an investment in property abroad to help your finances in later years. If you're starting a business or reducing your hours – and pay – at work, these circumstances may affect where you can afford to live. Let's look at a few of these circumstances and how you need to prepare yourself for making decisions about your property.

Making the most of an empty nest

So, the precious son or daughter made it to university after years of exams, trauma, arguments, worry and expense. Or your offspring have managed to get jobs that pay enough for them to move out of your home and become self-sufficient. Well, congratulations. You've done your job. This is what you were aiming for, right? So why do you feel bereft, abandoned, lost? Finally getting your house to yourself after two decades or more of hard work, noise and hassle can be a triumph or a trauma. Although your logical inner voice tells you that this is a great situation to be in, and you know deep down that this is absolutely the best thing for you and for your children, change is still very difficult to deal with. Suddenly becoming an 'empty nester' brings with it all sorts of changes. The silence in the house might be the first thing to strike you and this will carry on for 24 hours a day, every day. You will miss – believe it or not – the loud music, the noisy arguments and banter, the crashing doors at the end of arguments and the slam of the front door last thing at night when you know that the last of your offspring is finally home and safe. The house will even smell differently. No more will there be a waft of strong aftershave from the bathroom every evening or the smell of that unique blend of toiletries that your daughter uses. There will be no more smell of acrid smoke as sausages are grilled as an after-pub snack or the curry takeaway that has been brought back. You may even be able to see some carpet now that the oversized trainers are no longer left lying around or the CDs strewn about in the living room. Eventually, you will come to realise that you don't need to cook enough potatoes or pasta for four every time and your shopping habits will change. No more 'buy one get one free' offers on packs of 24 loo rolls or giant packs of cereal for you. You'll maybe start to buy the more expensive brand of coffee as you get used to the change and your shopping bill starts to drop. And that's the key to a successful empty nest. You need to see the advantages. As you sit contemplating a deserted house, missing your offspring's company, this may seem difficult but it's perfectly possible.

So, what are the advantages of having your home to yourself? Here are just a few:

- *Lack of worry* No more will you have to wait and worry if your children don't come home at the expected time. You may worry for a while after they've left home that they are staying out late, not eating properly and so on but you won't actually know when they are late home – or even stay out all night. Their leaving home really does signify the passage into adulthood and the hours they keep are no longer your problem.

- *Less expense* Undoubtedly your food and fuel bills will go down as soon as you (and your partner, if you have one) are left alone in the house. You will have to buy less of almost everything – bread, eggs, meat, loo rolls, biscuits and snacks. This is only true, of course, if you change your habits. If you insist on continuing to prepare enough potatoes for four people when there are only two of you left and then feeding the leftovers to the dog, then your shopping bill won't change much, so it may take some time to adjust. Your fuel bill will go down dramatically as there is a drastic cut in the number – and length – of showers being taken and the heating is not left on all night and so on.

- *Less work* If you've been in the habit of cooking meals for your offspring and their friends, or even of clearing up after their visits then you'll notice a lightening of your workload. If you've also been doing the laundry for your 'almost-adult' then your washing basket will suddenly seem remarkably empty – all the time. There will be no more dirty footprints in the hall, no more scummy rings around the bath that someone 'forgot' to wipe off and no more abandoned plates, dishes and mugs under the sofa. The few weeks after your son or daughter leaves home will show you just how much work one young person can generate. Be grateful you no longer have to do this.

- *Calm and quiet* At first this might seem to be a downside of an empty house but you will soon come to value the fact that no doors are being slammed and there are no arguments to sort out. When you live alone in your middle age, or as part of a couple, life can flow calmly along without any of the dramas you will have come to expect from the younger people in your life.

- *Freedom* Okay, you didn't exactly have to ask permission to do anything before your offspring flew the nest but you will undoubtedly feel a new sense of freedom now. You will be able to put your choice of music on the CD player or wander about naked if the mood takes you. Your sex life may well improve at this stage if you have previously felt inhibited by the presence of one or two sexually aware but cynical young people. You will no longer need to worry whether they have taken their key with them so you won't have to rush home to be there for them. You'll be able to eat and drink just what you want, when you want and the same applies to watching the television. Freedom is certainly something to be grateful for.

- *Getting your home back* When you share a home with someone, no matter how much you love them and enjoy their company, they are in your space. You may be surprised at just how much you value your own space.

- *Gaining a spare room* You now have a room within your home that does not have a permanent occupier. If your child has just gone to university and will be back for the odd weekend plus all the breaks, then not very much will change in this area, but if your child has gone off to permanent pastures new, then the room will be yours to do as you want with. What will you do with it? The options are almost unlimited. You could create a chill-out zone just for you, or a craft room where all the bits and pieces you need to make your greetings cards or sew clothing or soft furnishings could be stored. You could make the dream guest bedroom with glamorous new bed linen and tastefully arranged flowers – just like in the magazines. Or you could make a study or home office for yourself. At the very least it will give you somewhere that you can use for organised storage, thereby keeping the rest of the house uncluttered. The choice is yours, so make the most of it. Alternatively, you may decide that you no longer need all the space that your family home provides, and will consider moving to a smaller home. The next section will give you some information about this.

Considering downsizing

The traditional view of downsizing for older people is looking for a nice bungalow or a pretty little cottage, but there are lots of other options to be considered such as new-build properties or specially designed retirement apartments. Even if a bungalow or cottage sounds perfect for you, there are many things to take into account before making a decision of this magnitude.

There will be many motivating factors leading to a desire to downsize or to move house as you reach middle age. These could include the following:

- needing – or wanting – a different location: being near to the facilities offered by a town centre such as shops and regular activities or conversely, getting out of a busy town centre to a rural location or to the seaside may dictate a move
- wanting to live on one level so that stairs will not become a problem in later years: here a bungalow might be ideal or maybe an apartment (with a lift, of course)
- moving from an old property that demands a lot of attention to a newer property that will be easier to live in
- moving to be closer to family: when grandchildren start to arrive – as they often do in your middle years – you may well develop a burning desire to be closer so that you can enjoy your grandchildren's company more often or, just as likely, be on hand for babysitting duties. You might also think that being closer to family could be useful to you as you grow older and need some help yourself
- wanting a smaller – or bigger – garden: you might see your older years approaching and think that you won't be able to manage your present garden or, on the other hand, have a yearning for a bigger garden to keep you busy in the early years of your retirement
- a warmer climate: the desire to sell up and move to Spain or some other sunny, overseas destination can be overwhelming on a cold, grey morning in November but this sort of move requires plenty of thought as does any move that will take you away from friends, family and all things familiar. Think carefully, too, about your long-term plans. Very few people actually sell up, move to Spain or France and stay there living happily ever after. Most people come back to their roots eventually so it's a good idea to try to keep some sort of base in the UK as a back-up plan

- a reduction in maintenance: it's important to be able to keep your property in good condition whatever your age and if you can see that painting first-floor windows will become too much for you in the near future, then a move to a bungalow or somewhere with UPVC window frames would be a good idea to consider
- financial reasons: if your current property is a large one you may be able not only to benefit from smaller bills if you move to a smaller home but also to free up some capital by buying something less expensive
- needing less space: if you've been living in a family-sized home but no longer have family living with you, then now might be the right time to move.

Whatever your motives for moving house, it is not something you should undertake lightly. Moving house is an expensive and risky business. Solicitor's and Estate Agent's fees plus stamp duty, removal expenses, new carpets and curtains all add up so you must be sure that the new home is right for you. There are several things you can consider to help make sure that your decision is the right one.

- Make sure you've experienced the area you've chosen for your new home at different times and on different days. If you go to view the property on Sunday afternoon, that main road running past the front door may be quiet – but try it again in the rush hour. Things like market days or other regular events may also affect your new property, so do your research.
- Are you sure that you won't need the space in the future? Your family may have left home, but will you need space in your new home for them to stay when they visit or will you be able to accommodate the family for Christmas Dinner?
- Check out the facilities that are important to you. Do you often visit the library or the post office? Do you want to be able to walk to local shops? Are good transport links vital? Only you will be able to decide precisely what you need, but before you buy somewhere new you should think about how you live now and how you expect to live in the future. You can then make sure that you have covered all the things that will help to make your new life comfortable and successful.
- Think carefully about how important some of the things that you may currently take for granted may be when you are older. The garden may seem like a chore while you're still

working but may become a delight when you're retired. A spacious home may seem like it will be hard work for an older person but maybe you'll miss the space so it may be worth hanging on to it and arranging help with cleaning or maintenance.

- Do you really need the money that you could free up by moving to a smaller property? And are there other ways of freeing up that money? Equity release is something that can be a risky business in itself so professional advice is vital, but it may offer you a way to stay in your property in your old age if you love your home and don't really want to move.

- Look carefully at your financial situation. Is the mortgage on your current home paid off? If it is, then you might not want to take on another mortgage now. Or you might not be able to get a mortgage. Banks and building societies will, of course, only lend to people who they think will be able to pay them back. This might mean that you are offered a mortgage with a very short repayment term (and correspondingly higher monthly payments) so that it is repaid before your retirement or you may not be able to get a mortgage at all if you are already retired – or close to it – and do not have a substantial retirement income.

- If you are planning a move to be near your children, are they pretty certain to stay in the area to which you're moving? How awful would it be to sell a beloved family home simply to be nearer your offspring, only for them to get the job offer of a lifetime and up sticks themselves?

- Is there some aspect of your current home that you particularly love? Perhaps you relish breakfast in the conservatory or like having the convenience of an ensuite bathroom. If so, try not to move to somewhere that doesn't have this facility or where it cannot be added.

- Similarly, don't move to a place that is totally different in style to your current home unless you're convinced you're ready for the change. If you've been living in a large Victorian semi and are contemplating a move to a tiny, new, modern apartment, you may need to change not only your location but also all your furniture so that it will fit into your new home. You may find that not only will it not physically fit into the new property but also that the style is totally wrong. You will then have to factor in the cost of new furniture in addition to all the other expenses. You may also find the new style very unsettling.

- Finally, make sure that you have given a lot of time to considering how this will affect your social life. You will be moving away from friends and familiar activities and will also be losing your support network. If you have an active social life now, will you be able to build something similar in the place to which you're moving? Be careful not to underestimate how long this could take you and how you will feel in the meantime. Living in a new area can be a lonely experience, especially if you've been used to having lots of social contact and being able to call on people for help if you need it in an emergency – or when you simply need a sympathetic ear or an evening out.

If you are looking for a second home, whether in this country or abroad, you should be confident that you can manage two properties – both financially and physically. Be careful, in your first flush of enthusiasm for the idea, not to underestimate the costs of the upkeep of two homes, quite apart from the initial cost of purchase. For a property in this country, you may have two lots of council tax, TV licence, heating and lighting (you can't leave a property empty and unheated for long periods and security may dictate that you have some lights going on and off throughout the time when you are not there), the cost of someone to keep a check on your second property or to manage it for you plus the costs of general maintenance. For a property abroad you will have additional travelling costs on top of maintenance and service charges where appropriate. Keeping two properties going takes effort as well as money. Maintenance, cleaning and travelling all take time and you must decide if this will fit successfully into your life.

Whatever choice you make about your future home, make it carefully. Take your time and don't rush into anything. If the location is a big change for you – going to live abroad or to the opposite end of the country, for example, try renting first or at least have an extended stay there. Avoid changing your whole lifestyle based on just a week or two on holiday or odd days spent looking around an area for houses. Try to take into account all the possible costs of a move and make sure that you really are getting what you want. Acting in haste will very rarely result in the perfect move.

Property abroad

Buying a property abroad has become increasingly popular in recent years and, according to the Office of National Statistics, the British now own over a quarter of a million foreign properties – twice as many as ten years ago. This growth has been prompted by several changes in our society – the uncertainty regarding financial products causing us to look at alternative ways of financing our retirements, the advent and increasing popularity of low-cost airlines and the ever-increasing adventurousness of the over 50s, looking for ways to spend their leisure time.

Of course, we've all fallen in love with a pretty place that we've seen while we've been on holiday and we've all looked in the estate agents' windows, checking out the prices, dreaming of an escape. However, buying a property abroad is far from an easy move to make whether you intend to live abroad permanently, are buying as an investment or are simply buying somewhere to spend your holidays in the sun. There are lots of issues to consider and decisions to be made. First you need to be clear about why you are buying abroad and to be sure that it is the right thing for you to do. Consider the following:

- *What will you be giving up?* Will you be happy to be living perhaps thousands of miles away from your family and friends? Remember that moving a great distance will mean that you are unable to carry on the social life that you may have built up over a number of years – you will be starting from scratch in your new location.
- *Pensions and finances* Check out your state pension entitlement and whether it will be possible for it to be paid to you in your country of choice. Will your financial situation fully cover all the costs involved in moving to a foreign country?
- *Language issues* Are you prepared to put in the time and effort to learn a new language? If you're just going to use your new property for occasional holidays, then you will probably be able to get away with learning just a few words to smooth your way in restaurants and so on and will be able to hire translators or English-speaking experts to help you with finding your way through the buying process. But if you intend to spend long periods abroad – perhaps envisaging yourself spending winters in a warmer climate – then you will need to conquer the local language so that you can take your

place in society. If you are unable to communicate with the people where you are living, then life could be a bit difficult at best. You could find yourself socially isolated and unable to conduct even routine business.

Of course, the major decision that has to be made once you have set your heart on buying abroad is where you will buy this property. You may have decided upon the country but there are still lots of things to take into consideration in deciding the exact location including:

- your budget, which will often dictate where and what you are able to buy – make sure that you've allowed for the legal, viewing and moving expenses
- proximity to an airport
- town or country?
- a rural or coastal setting?
- local amenities – including shops, banks, bars and restaurants, sports facilities and entertainment
- health care facilities
- how far from your nearest neighbours?
- is there employment available locally if you will need to work?
- how big a property do you need or can you afford?
- is it to be purely for your own personal use, for occasional use, to include family coming to stay or will you be renting the property out. If you're looking for a rental income, how much are similar properties being rented out for locally?

Wherever you decide to buy a property and no matter what that property is like, it is vital that you proceed carefully. Expert advice is of the utmost importance. Buying a property in the UK is fraught with unforeseen dangers even though we are relatively familiar with the system and are fluent in the language. We can all tell our horror stories of things that have gone wrong when we're moving house. Imagine how much more difficult it must be to buy a property in a country where we don't really know the system or where we don't understand the language. Having someone who can explain to you exactly what each document that you are being asked to sign says and who can steer you through the system is invaluable. You will need to deal with reputable estate agents and to get a good, English-speaking lawyer situated in the country where you're buying. There are all sorts of pitfalls that experts can help you to avoid. Just to take one example, in Spain, where many Brits buy property, you must make a will in Spanish before you will be allowed to complete the property-buying process. So, be warned – take care when buying abroad, do your research, make sure that it is right for you and that you have enlisted the help of all the appropriate, well-qualified experts.

Jane and Ken's story

Jane and Ken were in their early 50s and, when their younger daughter went to university, were typical empty-nesters. They found themselves with lots more time to sit together in the evenings and talk about things they had not touched on for decades. They discovered – to their mutual surprise – that they both dreamed of owning a cottage in France. It had been many years since they had taken their holidays in France but during the cold winter evenings after their daughter had left home they planned several weekends in different parts of France for the following spring and summer. During these weekends they agreed on an area of Brittany that they loved and started to search in earnest for a suitable property. They eventually bought a rundown farmhouse that they spent many months refurbishing – rediscovering between them, along the way, a love of DIY and interior design. They now spend most holidays in Brittany and are planning to spend at least half the year there when they retire in a few years' time. The conversations they had as empty-nesters led to them investing in a property abroad and finding a new lease of life as a couple.

Maintenance – now and in the future

While you're in your 50s, problems with home maintenance are more likely to involve cost, inconvenience or hard work. If cost is an issue then the obvious solution is to do it yourself. You may have a steep learning curve ahead of you if you've not had much DIY experience but friends may help out so that you can learn from them or you may be able to swap skills. If you're good at painting but can't tackle electrical repairs then get together with appropriate friends and get a swap system organised. The problem of inconvenience caused by major repairs or alterations to your property will just have to be put up with, while the only remedy for hard work is paying someone else to do it for you. Finding reputable and reliable tradesmen is a perennial problem so ask around for recommendations and then treat the good ones that you do find very well indeed.

Maintaining your property in later years can be even more problematical. Then the problems could well include the same financial shortfalls but your tolerance for inconvenience will probably be reduced. It can be difficult to cope with a set of builders in the house with the attendant dust, rubble and mess if you are unsteady on your feet. Doing it yourself may not be an option in old age so repairs and alterations could become almost impossible. For these reasons it is vital that while you're fit and able – i.e. while you're in your 50s – you get your property in absolutely tip-top condition. Neglecting essential repairs now may be saving you time and money that will bring short-term rewards, but you will be storing up trouble for the future. It is also important that you think of the future when you're making alterations to your property. A spiral staircase to the upper floor or to a loft extension may seem like an attractive and viable option for the next few years but are you sure you'll be able to cope with it in 15 or 20 years time? A generous staircase now may be a bit of an expense but in years to come you'll have forgotten the builder's bill that you got and will be able to use the upper floors of your home with ease. A little thought now will pay dividends later.

Summary

In this chapter we've looked at property matters including the advantages of your children leaving home and how this might affect how you use your property. We've also considered the pros and cons of downsizing – something that might be prompted by your children leaving home – such as saving money on maintenance and running costs and moving away from an area that is familiar for you. If you're staying put, then maintaining your property will be important and we've looked at how to consider how to do this now and in the future when it may become more of a problem for you. Finally, we looked at some of the pitfalls that you must be aware of and decisions that you will have to make if you are buying a property abroad.

Action plan: home maintenance and improvement

Take a good look around your home – including all the external aspects, garden, garage, paths and so on. Is it in perfect condition with nothing likely to need doing for years? Very few of us will be able to answer an honest 'Yes' to that question so you should make a list of all the things that need doing. Try to think to the future while you're making your list. If you know that the front door, for example, will last for another year or two but will need replacing soon, note that in your long-term plans. Include all the jobs, no matter how small – such as wonky door handles, dripping taps, a central heating boiler that has already broken down more than once – and finally consider how often redecoration will be necessary. You can then prioritize this list so that you know exactly what your property needs and when you will have to do it. Try to put at the top of your list for action all the things that are currently in need of repair and which, if left, could cause damage or get worse in time, resulting in a more serious and more costly repair. A dripping tap would come into this category as would missing or loose tiles on the roof as both could result in further damage to your property.

Now work through your list in your spare time. If money is not an issue, you will be able to engage tradesmen to bring your home up to standard, but if you're on a budget, then you may want to tackle the jobs yourself.

The idea of compiling a list like this is so that as you approach retirement your property is in tip-top condition and there will not be any nasty surprises for you that mean that your finances are stretched or that jobs you could tackle yourself in your 50s become a real problem in your 70s.

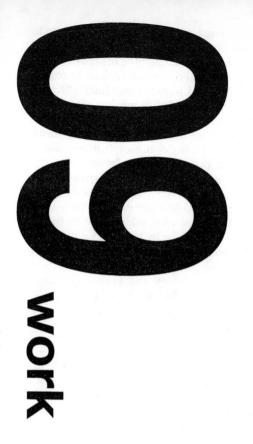

09

work

In this chapter you will learn:
- how to assess your prospects
- how to avoid ageism
- how to change direction.

Something strange happens to many people in their employment when they reach mid-life. It is not a mid-life crisis, it is more of a desire for change, a questioning that often takes place at this time. We start to challenge ourselves, asking lots of questions such as 'Is this all there is?', 'Am I happy doing this?', 'What's next?' or 'Can I do better than this?' We often come to the realisation that we didn't actually choose to do the job we're doing but drifted into it when we were much younger, for all sorts of reasons, and that maybe it doesn't suit us any more. Lots of people go through this and react by starting the countdown to retirement as a way of escaping their frustration and boredom. Some will simply resign themselves to their situation and 'switch off' from work, then develop their lives outside work to compensate. Others will take action to find a way out of the area of work they are in by looking for different opportunities, taking courses or by starting their own businesses. Of course, there are people to whom this does not happen and they will continue to enjoy and progress in their careers. But I have observed this phenomenon happening to many people around the time they reach their 50s as they come to realize that they have reached the peak of their earning power and that younger people are taking over the workplace.

What are your prospects?

As we touched on in the previous section, reaching your 50s often triggers a questioning of just where we are and where we are going in our careers. It can be a time of great change or a time of consolidation. Whether you are looking for a major change in your working life or simply wanting to improve your prospects in terms of your present position, you should not let age get in the way. We live in a society where younger is often put forward as being better than older but, especially in terms of employment, this is just not true. The majority of jobs require a variety of skills. They do not just require the two types of skill that may be affected by age – physical and cognitive skills – they need a blend of skills and aptitudes including planning, motivation, prioritising, organising and problem solving. These latter skills are not ones that are affected negatively by ageing; in fact these get better with the experience that age brings. It therefore follows that some jobs will be done better by older rather than younger workers, so prospects should not necessarily deteriorate as we reach mid-life.

Having accepted that we have just as much – if not more – to offer as a younger worker, we can review our prospects realistically. Consider the following:

- *Experience* At this stage in your life you will have plenty of this to offer. Make sure that your employer knows about it. Use job reviews and appraisal situations to put forward your case. Ask about opportunities that may be coming up and fit your experience to the situation.

- *Skills and aptitudes* Things such as organisational skills, loyalty, stability, maturity, ability to remain calm under pressure and practical knowledge accumulated over years are valuable to any employer and it is up to you to make sure that your employer appreciates what you have to offer.

- *What you really want* This requires you to ask some searching questions of yourself. Are you happy with your current position? Do you want more responsibility – or less? Are you too familiar – and bored – with your daily routine? How much extra effort are you prepared to put in to gain promotion or advancement? Are you doing your job just for the money or do you enjoy it?

- *Your employer's situation* Are there opportunities for advancement in your present job? Is the organisation doing well? Is it expanding? Is it a good firm to work for?

- *Your financial situation* Do you need more income? If this is the reason for chasing promotion, then you will have to accept that hard work will be required. You should also consider whether there is a good pension scheme with your current employer and if so, how a move to another company or a promotion within the current company might affect your entitlement.

A thorough review of your current situation and of what you really want or need from your employment will help you to assess your prospects and to decide what actions you should take in both the short and medium terms. Ensuring that your employers fully understand what you are offering and what you require in return is essential and this self-assessment is an important first step in getting to where you want to be.

One of the main problems faced by mid-life workers looking to continue the progress in their careers is ageism and we will look at the effects this has in the next section.

Ageism and how to avoid it

Ageism is discrimination based on chronological age and the use of age to define capabilities and roles. You may find that your employer does not offer you the same opportunities for training or development, thinking that you're 'past it', or you may be overlooked for promotion. Or you find yourself first in line for redundancy. You may find yourself discriminated against when you're looking for a job and come to feel that all the attractive-sounding jobs are aimed at much younger people. There is evidence of age discrimination in job adverts against people as young as 35 and the Age Concern ICM Poll of December 2001 estimated that 1.8 million people between the ages of 55 and 64 will be affected by ageism in the workplace. At the time of writing, new legislation is imminent in the UK aimed at defeating ageism in employment but, until we see how that will work to help us, there are actions you can take now if you are a victim of age discrimination at work.

- Approach your boss and ask if you are being discriminated against. It is likely that, in the atmosphere of increased awareness of ageism that accompanies the new legislation, this will be sufficient to worry your employers and they may put the situation right straight away.

- If they need some convincing to give you the same opportunities as younger people, try pointing out to them that younger staff are more likely to leave before the employer has benefited from the training – they actually stay an average of only two years after receiving training. If you're in your early 50s you are far more likely to stay and allow your employer to get the benefit of any training they give you.

- Point out the advantages of a mix of ages in the workforce (higher retention rates, lower absenteeism, increased motivation, greater flexibility and a wider pool of skills). The Government's 'Code of Practice for Age Diversity in Employment' (available in PDF format from the Age Positive website www.agepositive.gov.uk) gives some guidelines for employers to help them eliminate ageism in matters such as recruitment, redundancy, training and promotion.

- Sell yourself. Make sure your employers know about all the things you've done to develop yourself (include voluntary work, courses you've taken in your own time and so on) and that they are aware of the extent of the experience you have in their business.

- If you're finding it difficult to get a job because of your age, try contacting the Third Age Employment Network (www.taen.org.uk) who can put you in touch with some specialist employment agencies for older workers.

There undoubtedly has been a lot of age discrimination in employment – and this can apply to younger people too, although admittedly to a lesser degree, when they are judged to be too young to be worth promoting – but there is a lot of hope that this will start to decrease when the new legislation becomes accepted and attitudes change. In the meantime, we can all help ourselves by being aware of the opportunities that are around us and speaking out if we feel we're being passed over.

Being an asset

One way of ensuring that we are more likely to be fairly treated at work is to make our employers see us as an asset to their business. Of course, older, more experienced workers are assets but in recent decades there has been an increasingly prevalent view that youth is best. Many employers see older workers as having inherent problems such as the greater chance of illness disrupting the business, a slowing down of thought processes and a decrease in physical strength plus possible problems caused by sight and hearing problems. However, although some of these things are undoubtedly true in some cases, nobody has noticed – and certainly have not proved – lower productivity in the workplace with age. In fact, the opposite is true. Many studies have shown that the group of workers with the lowest productivity are those aged 25 or under. So, the task for us over-50s is not just to become proficient at our jobs – an asset to any business – but also to find a way of making this obvious to our employers.

Many studies, measuring performance in the workplace and also based on the perceptions of managers, have found lots of advantages of older workers. These include:

- experience – the obvious one
- fewer accidents – we're just more sensible
- harder working – we've worked in a different age to this one
- more effective – we've learned what works
- better motivated – any group of people who find themselves discriminated against tends to work harder to prove themselves

- better interpersonal skills – lifelong learning can give us these skills
- less likely to leave – we know how difficult it might be to get another job at our age
- lower rates of absenteeism – despite the reputation for having lots of aches and pains, we tend to see the importance of turning up regularly.

Your job is to convince your boss of all these advantages of your being an older worker. Make sure that your achievements – meeting targets, good attendance record, highest sales or throughput in the department, length of service and so on – are well documented and also volunteer to participate in a mentoring scheme or even suggest one if such a thing does not exist to help younger workers in your company. If you carry out volunteer work in your spare time or have taken courses of study that will either be directly relevant to your work or will have contributed to your personal development, then make sure that your personnel records reflect this. Bring these matters up during your annual appraisal review. In short, blow your own trumpet, don't be modest, let them know just who you are and how valuable to them you are.

Managing a younger boss

As you go through your career it is almost inevitable that at some point – especially near the end of your working life – you will have to report to a younger boss. You may be lucky and get an enlightened one: someone who knows the value of older workers and will treat you just as well as they treat people of their own age. If you are unfortunate enough to get a boss who truly believes that younger workers are better and deserve better opportunities for promotion, training or just the more interesting projects in the department, then it will again be up to you to educate them. Read through the information and suggestions in the previous section and put them into practice.

In addition to these suggestions, it may help to try to understand their point of view. Young managers might be feeling insecure and will be anxious to make an impression. The older worker, with the benefit of greater experience should be able to defuse any tension by making it clear that they are not trying to challenge any decisions the younger manager might make. It could also help to go out of your way to ask your boss for advice and guidance as this will reinforce the impression that you are just like any other worker that the boss has to manage. It is important not to come across as patronizing or resentful. Do not let your boss see you as a threat and, finally, don't act your age. As the usual view of older workers is of people who are slow, inflexible and resistant to change, try to show enthusiasm and energy and to accept change cheerfully.

A change of direction – it's not too late

The previous sections have all been about making the most of your current employment, but what if you are hopelessly dissatisfied at work and yearn for a change? As we said right at the start of this book, when you enter your 50s you have a couple of decades of active life in front of you and you need to make the most of it. There can be few worse fates in terms of employment than working for 10 years or more at a job you hate, where every day is a trial and you're just counting down the hours to when you can stop working. Don't do it. Take a change of direction while you still have time. Don't stay stuck in a rut – there are lots of options in this situation.

- Find another job in a similar field – and remember that there will be legislation to help you with ageism. Don't put your date of birth on the application form or on your CV – it's irrelevant. Employers will be able to guess at your age from your employment history but you don't have to help them to be ageist.
- Ask if you can go part-time or work out a job share. Working fewer hours might be all it takes to give you your life back and make you feel more in control.
- Take early retirement if it's feasible. See Chapter 10 for help on when and how to retire early.
- Start your own business – see Chapter 12 for more information.
- Do something completely different. Think about all the things you enjoy and/or have been good at over the years and try to find a job with some sort of connection with these things. You may have to accept a lower salary but if you think carefully you may feel it is well worth it.

Check out all your options and take your courage in both hands then take the leap. People who make big changes at this time in their lives rarely regret it.

Summary

In this chapter we have looked at how age can affect our working lives. Ageism is a major problem in the workplace. So much so that the government has developed legislation to help to deal with it. Attitudes will be slow to change though and in the meantime, as we have seen, the over-50s must survive and thrive in society as it is right now. Many workers will face problems at work in mid-life and we have looked at how we can deal with issues such as a change of direction, having a younger boss and feelings of frustration or boredom in our jobs so that we can continue to get the most out of life.

Action plan: keeping happy at work

Sometimes being happy is all about appreciating what we have. Your task in this action plan is to list all the good things about your job.

If you're now thinking, but I hate it, there's nothing good about it, then you must either think harder or change your job – or maybe both.

There are a number of items to think about and perhaps include in your list of things to appreciate about your current position.

- *Hours* Do you do as many, or as few hours as you need?
- *Location* Is it handy for home, or the shops at lunchtime?
- *Colleagues* Are there any people at work that you would consider to be friends. Perhaps you see them outside work too?
- *Social life* Are there social opportunities attached to your job? Perhaps there is an active social club financed by your employer or the staff organise outings and events for themselves.
- *Prestige* If it's a well-respected job, you may get a lot of satisfaction out of that or the work may be a part of who you are.
- *Your salary* Unless you're in the fortunate position of not needing to earn any money, then this must be one of the good things about your job. If you would like – or need – more money, then you will have to work out a solution involving perhaps a change of employer or promotion.
- *The job itself* What do you do on a day-to-day basis? Is some of it enjoyable, rewarding or interesting?

If you can think of even a few advantages of having the job you've got and remind yourself of them on a daily basis, then you will have gone a long way, by 'counting your blessings', to making yourself happy at work.

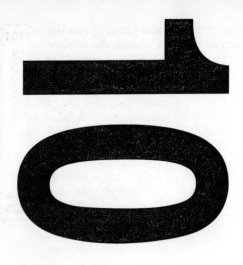

10
work/life balance

In this chapter you will learn:
- some ways to reduce your working hours
- how to decide when to retire
- how to develop new interests.

The work/life balance is a much talked-about issue. When the baby boomers were busy bringing up their children, the issue of balancing work and 'life' was not mentioned. We just had to get on with it. Now, at the start of the twenty-first century, it's an issue that everyone cares about. It is now widely agreed that young mothers need 'me time' and young fathers need to spend time with their children and we are all encouraged to check whether we have achieved a balance between the time and effort that we spend on our employment and the time and effort we spend on the rest of our life. In the 1980s in particular, a work culture developed that involved longer and longer hours spent at work and the stress that work involved could severely impinge on the rest of life. It may be that today's 50 to 60-year-olds are still suffering from that culture as they would have been forging their careers in the 1980s. For the benefit of our health and the happiness of our families, it is essential that we extricate ourselves from the mindset that says long hours at work are acceptable and that working until you have no energy, time or inclination for a satisfying home life is normal behaviour.

No matter how imperative the extra hours and effort at work seem, there are ways to change your working patterns to ensure that you have time to live – and enjoy – a life outside work. By the time you've reached your 50s, you will probably have reached a peak in your career and it may be possible to stop the relentless push for promotion that might have been a dominating feature of your working life in your younger years. However, a consequence of this continued push for progress in your career is that habits become set. Although your working hours may be, for example, 9 to 5, you may have become fixed in getting to work at 8 and not leaving until after everyone else has left at 6 or 7 p.m. This habit can be changed, although it may be necessary to cut down gradually. Try, for instance, committing yourself to meeting up with friends for a drink or a game of badminton or golf on one evening each week. Make sure the time arranged necessitates leaving work at 5 p.m. And if you have a late night, go in to work a little later the following morning. With determination, you will be able to establish new habits and will end up with a better work/life balance.

Of course, a change in mindset is needed in addition to the change in hours worked. Realising that work is just one part of life and putting work in its place is essential. You may have to ask yourself some searching questions if you are in a situation where you not only work long hours but also bring work home with you and worry about work-related matters at the weekend.

If you have frequently allowed work commitments to come before family occasions then you will need to decide now, in your 50s, what is really important to you. As the old adage goes, 'very few people on their deathbed wish they had spent more time at work', so put yourself, your family and friends before work for a change and you will be nearer to finding that elusive work/life balance.

Part time or full time?

Depending on your finances and the type of work you do, there may be even greater opportunities to alter your work/life balance in favour of less work and more life. There are a number of ways in which you can reduce the number of hours of paid employment that you undertake each week:

- Simply ask your current employers if you can reduce your hours. Explain to them that you want to spend time on other things and point out the benefits for them – paying you less, improved performance, retention of an experienced worker and so on. It may be possible to work one or two days per week less so that you have whole days free for other interests or you may prefer to change your starting and finishing times so that you miss rush-hour traffic, reducing a major source of stress in your life.

- Check out the situation as regards job sharing. See if your employers would be open to this and also check with friends and acquaintances to see if any of them would be suitable for sharing a job with you. This can be a particularly attractive option as it can keep you in a job you like and are good at while reducing the responsibility, stress and time spent at work.

- Consider a complete change of career. Wanting to work fewer hours does not necessarily mean that you have to carry on doing the type of job you've always done. There may be part-time opportunities in other areas such as delivery jobs, retail or catering, for example.

- Self-employment can be an option for people looking for part-time work. Obviously, if a business is simply a means of providing part-time employment for yourself you will not want to risk too much of your capital on such a venture, but there are several low-investment ideas you could consider, such as making use of existing skills in after-dinner speaking, consultancy, illustration or private tuition. There is plenty more information about self-employment in Chapter 12.

When to retire – and how

There are two totally opposing viewpoints on the age at which we should retire. Some people have worked all their lives and see retirement as the 'great escape'. They can't wait for the time when they can leave work behind and set out on that grand adventure known as retirement and they will plan their finances and their working life with the sole aim of getting out early and wouldn't dream of working until the statutory retirement age. Others bitterly resent there being any statutory retirement age at all. They can't imagine anything worse than, as they see it, sitting at home all day with nothing to do. Whichever camp you fall into, you will have to make plans to ensure that you can do exactly what suits you in terms of when you retire.

If you have plans to retire earlier than the age at which you are due to collect either your state pension or your occupational pension then there is obviously a lot you will have to do to get yourself into a position where that is possible. Your financial situation will have to be such that you will be able to live without your salary – more information about savings and financial planning in Chapter 13. You will also have to make plans as to what you will do with your time when you retire. Of course, there might be something that you are burning to do and having to work for a living has not allowed you the time to do it and this may be the driving force behind your desire to retire early. In this case it will be easy to put things in place so that you can get on with it as soon as you are free of work. This may be a yearning to travel the world for extended periods and you may be able to plan a grand trip to celebrate your retirement, for example, or you may want to spend more time on an existing hobby and you will naturally slot into this way of life as soon as you leave work. But if, on the other hand, you just want to be out of a work situation then you must be careful not to over-glamorize the life you will be leading after retirement. You will have to be sure that you will not be bored at home. There will be more about developing new interests in retirement in the next section. The other thing you will have to do if you want to retire early is to set up the arrangements at work. Some employers are glad to get rid of older workers so that they can fill the position with a younger, cheaper recruit. Others value older workers more highly and you may find that your employer is reluctant to let you go. If you are dependent upon claiming your occupational pension early to fund your retirement this may make things difficult and some negotiation may be necessary.

If you're in the camp that wants to work for as long as possible then you will still have to do some planning. Your employers may have a strict policy of retiring all workers as soon as they become eligible for their pension and you may have to leave that employer and find alternative work elsewhere. Do not let this daunt you if you really want to carry on working as there are lots of opportunities around – you just have to keep an open mind and search them out. There will also be decisions to be made regarding your finances, as there are advantages to be had if you defer taking the state retirement pension for even a short while. Also, if you just want to keep your regular contact with fellow-workers (the social side of working, for example) but would be able to manage financially with a lower, but regular, salary then you may be able to organise part-time employment – see the previous section for more details.

Whether your retirement is forced or voluntary, early or late, sooner or later you will leave your employment and start upon the next stage of your life and there are a number of practical and emotional things that will accompany this leave-taking. Usually you will have to engage in some sort of disentanglement from your job. This could involve passing on the rudiments of your job to the person who will replace you. This might be a relief if you are desperate to be rid of your duties or it might reinforce your feelings of loss, depending on your attitude to leaving. Another practical aspect to leaving might be packing up the personal belongings with which you have surrounded yourself – your diary and books, pens and the odd pot plant. Putting these few things into a cardboard box might just bring forth an unexpected emotional response. Despite appearances, remember that these sparse belongings do not represent your contribution to the whole of society for your entire working life. Your work is less tangible but will probably have been far more valued and anyway, you've been paid for it. Don't allow yourself, at this stage, to become unduly sentimental or nostalgic about your job.

Another opportunity for sentimentality – or revenge perhaps – is the 'leaving do'. You may have to organise (or have organised for you) a get-together for your soon-to-be-ex-colleagues. This could range from a full-blown reception if you held a senior position for many years, to a drink on your last day at the local pub if you decide upon something less formal. Whatever sort of event is planned, you will need to prepare for the call to 'say a few words'. Try to resist this opportunity to tell your bosses where they have been going wrong all these years. Keep it simple, try to incorporate a few gentle jokes about the working environment and don't forget to thank the people with whom you've been working closely. If you really can't think of some pleasant things to say about the job you're leaving, concentrate on what your life will involve after retirement – perhaps by letting your colleagues know what sort of interests and activities you are planning to enjoy.

All of these things have the potential to bring out some surprising emotions. As you consider what you are leaving behind and what you are heading towards, your thoughts may turn to both good and bad things about your job. But the decision is made now and your new job is to look forward – and enjoy yourself.

Developing new interests

This is it. Your new life. Your chance to start enjoying some 'me time'. So, what will your new life be like? If you've been approaching your retirement without a thought as to what will occupy your time and have assumed that stopping working means that you'll finally have some time to sit down and do nothing, you may be in for a shock. Most retirees say, within just a few months of their retirement, that they don't know how they found time to go to work. It seems that some people just settle into a new routine without problems but, in reality, these are probably the people who give some thought to what they will do with the freedom of retirement well before it arrives. They will probably have spent months, if not years, developing their interests and imagining what they will do with their time.

If you are in your 50s you probably have plenty of time to plan for your retirement but you must not leave it too long before you start to lay out your ideas and put your plans for using your free time into action. Remember that your retirement will be the first time when you have been fully in control of your own time. There will be no one to insist that you arrive at a certain place by 8 or 9 a.m., no one to tell you what to do or when to do it. You must decide and it is important for your future happiness that you make your decisions with care to ensure that what you do in your retirement is really 'you'. Think hard about what gives you pleasure and satisfaction. Don't just think 'oh, I want a lie-in' or 'I want to do absolutely nothing' because they will soon become boring and certainly won't fill your days with joy and contentment. Maybe you want more time to spend with your partner or your grandchildren – but what activities will you do with them? Or maybe you've got a real desire to learn something new – so what will it be? The following are a few things you could consider.

- *Travel* There may be a whole list of places that you wish to see or maybe there is just one romantic place that it has been a long-held ambition of yours to see. Make sure you make the most of your active years to do the long haul, energetic holidays that you pine for.

- *Days out* If you spend all your free time at the moment catching up with household chores and organising your life ready for the Monday morning grind to begin again, then retirement is when you will be able to discover your local area and also go a little further afield for the day. There are many interesting things to see and do, right on our doorsteps, and you will have the luxury of being able to have days out without the weekend crowds.

- *Craft hobbies* You may want to learn something new or simply to spend more time on a hobby that you've always dabbled in. You may want to learn how to make jewellery or paint watercolours or make ceramics and almost certainly you will find a class to suit you at your local college (and don't forget that pensioners are often given reduced rates). If you want to devote more time to an existing hobby such as sewing clothes for yourself or your grandchildren then retirement is certainly the time of your life when you will be able to do this.

- *Sports* Go lf is the traditional pastime for retirees and, indeed, they usually get preferential fees for golf-club membership. However, this is something that you could start to play long before you retire. You might not be able to play very often, but is as well to check it out before you expect to spend day after day playing it. In fact, sports of any kind – including fishing, badminton, bowls, tennis, archery, running or rowing – are usually things that you will have done for a while before retirement. If you haven't been involved in a sport before you reach your retirement date, ask yourself 'why not?' Maybe it's because you don't really want to do it. So try it now before you're depending on it to use up your free time.

- *Getting fit* We've all done it – resolved to join a gym and really get fit but never got around to it. Some of us have even gone ahead and joined a gym and then never got the tracksuit and trainers out. Maybe, when retirement is a reality, your determination to get fit will finally find an outlet.

- *DIY* If you've been putting off jobs that need doing around the house, then maybe retirement is the time when you will finally 'get your house in order'.
- *Voluntary work* Now may be your chance to 'put something back' into society. There is more on this in Chapter 14.

Whatever you decide to do in retirement, especially if you are taking early retirement, make sure you do something. This is the time of your life and should be when some of your dreams can come true. Try to find a wide variety of occupations, as even the most beloved hobby will pale if you spend every day doing it – and you wouldn't want to spoil your enjoyment of something that is dear to you simply because you haven't thought of anything else you want to do, would you? Another important bit of advice is to get out of the house. You may want to spend day after day pottering around at home, simply because you see this as something that you haven't had much time for in the past, but resist the temptation. There will be plenty of time for sitting at home in later decades or when the weather is awful, so make the most of any opportunity to get out and about. It is only by getting out of your comfort zone that you will find new friends, new interests, new happiness and a new life.

Family time

One thing a lot of people aim to do in retirement is to spend more time with their families. A straw poll of a group of 50-plus mothers that I mentioned previously said that the greatest advantage of being over 50 was grandchildren, so this is often the first aim of new retirees – to spend more time with their grandchildren.

In some cases there may be little choice in this, as offspring may need help with childcare to allow them to fulfil their work commitments. Unless you are desperate to look after your grandchildren on a daily basis, take care about making a commitment like this. It could mean that you are simply swapping one type of work commitment for another and your dream of freedom may disappear amid a pile of nappies and the school run. It does, of course, bring with it rewards of an entirely different kind to paid employment and you may find that forming a close relationship with your grandchildren while at the same time helping your children turns out to be the best thing you've ever done. Doing a trial run, perhaps taking your last week or two of annual leave to do it, may be the best way to see if it is for you.

There are other members of your family with whom you may wish – or need – to spend more time, and starting to work part time or retiring from work altogether may help in this aim. If you want to spend more time with your partner – and perhaps he or she has retired before you – then retiring will be a good move. You will be able to get out and about when the roads are quieter, i.e. when the rest of the world is at work or school (although you may be surprised just how many people are out shopping or at the gym on weekday mornings) and you will be able to potter about the house together instead of racing around getting ready for work or getting all the chores done.

Another group of people you may need to spend more time with is elderly relatives. Here again you should take care before making a major commitment of your time. Although very old people may seem forgetful at times, you can be sure they will not forget if you say you will 'pop round every morning, when I retire'. Think carefully about exactly how much care they need and weigh up all the alternatives (paying an agency, sharing duties with other relatives, sheltered housing, Social Services, care homes, etc.) before taking on the lion's share of the duties yourself. Find more information in Chapter 7, which concentrates on the options and on looking after the older generation.

Summary

In this chapter we've looked at how you will spend your time in your 50s. Sometimes the importance of work can diminish and also, as you progress in your 50s, you will begin to be very aware that you are approaching retirement. This, perhaps combined with your children having left home, can result in your having extra time for yourself in your 50s and you need to be very sure that you do not waste any of this very valuable, enjoyable decade. There are lots of things that you can do with your time rather than just having a lie-in – ranging from spending more time with your family to developing hobbies, sports and pastimes, getting fit or doing some voluntary work.

When to retire and how to make your escape is something that needs careful consideration and plenty of planning – from financial preparations to winding down your commitments at work.

Whatever your attitude to retirement – can't wait for it to come or dreading it – you will need to plan for it if you are to make the most of it. It is essential to keep in mind that it does not signify the end of your useful life, merely the start of another stage.

Action plan: being happy with your balance

We all have the same amount of time available to us – 168 hours every week – but some people seem so much happier with how they use their time. The trick is to work out a work/life balance with which we are content. If we're using too much of our time for things that do not give us satisfaction, then we will never find that elusive balance. Our action plan to ensure we arrive at a work/life balance that is right for us involves the following steps.

- List the things that you have to do each week and the amount of time you estimate that you spend doing them – include things like work, travelling to work, jobs you have to do at home, preparing meals each day, washing and ironing and so on.
- Now list the things that you like to do. Here you can write down all those things that you do for pleasure such as meeting friends, hobbies and sports, spending time with your partner, chatting on the phone – whatever you love to do – and again note how much time you spend doing these things.
- Compare your lists. If you've got too much on your 'have to do' list, then see where you can cut down on your commitments. If you've not got much on your 'love to do' list, ask yourself why not? Is it because you don't have many hobbies or that you feel you don't have enough time for these things? Only you can review your own situation realistically, but remember that you're aiming at a balance between the two lists. If there are things that appear on both lists – for example, you might feel that you 'have' to exercise, but have put going to the gym on your 'love to do' list, then delete it from your 'have to do' list.

- Keep a diary. Don't use it just for work and dental appointments; put everything in so that spending an hour on the phone catching up with friends or going for a game of golf is given equal importance with work or other commitments.
- Learn to say 'no'. Look at your list of things that you feel you have to do. Are there lots of things on there that you do for other people but that you resent because they take away time that you could spend on things you like doing? Refusing to take on further commitments or telling people that 'You would love to keep helping them but are too busy just now' will free up some time and lower your stress levels.
- Take action. The old adage of 'if you do what you've always done, you'll get what you've always got' is true in this situation. To improve your work/life balance you must understand your current situation (and the lists will help with that) and then do something about what you find.

A work/life balance that suits you will improve your life. Everybody's priorities and requirements in this are different but if you can get it right for you then happiness will be yours. If you do what you love and value then success is guaranteed.

11

redundancy

In this chapter you will learn:

- how to view redundancy as an opportunity
- how to consider all your options
- some advice on getting back into the workforce.

Although we looked at problems relating to our working lives in Chapter 9, a separate chapter is devoted to the issue of redundancy simply because it causes particular problems for older workers. Finding a new job after redundancy can be more difficult for people over 50. This is due to ageism, which we discussed in Chapter 9. A recent study found that ageism was the most common form of prejudice in the UK – more common than even sexism or racism. When you're over 50 and applying for a job, this can be devastating. There are many cases of well-qualified and well-experienced people in their 50s applying for hundreds of jobs and getting very few interviews. How we deal with redundancy then, can have an affect on our lives, so we must learn the tricks that will help us to make a success of our working lives – even if this involves coping with redundancy.

A threat – or an opportunity?

How we view a problem can have a noticeable affect on how well we cope with it. If we feel constantly under threat of redundancy and are always looking over our shoulders, waiting for the axe to fall and assessing our chances compared with those of our younger colleagues, then our working lives will be miserable. The threat of redundancy will eat away at our self-confidence and come to dominate our every thought – not just at work but at home too, causing stress to build up and every area of our lives to be affected. If we see it as something inevitable, a terrible event to be feared, with nothing we can do about it, then it will definitely get us down.

If you can view redundancy as a possible opportunity we are far more likely to get positive results – and to enjoy ourselves far more in the process. It is important to keep a sense of perspective in this situation and, it can't be said often enough, to consider all your options. Redundancy is not a sure-fire disaster in your life. It can have positive effects, even if they are not immediately apparent. Being made redundant may give you an invaluable opportunity to think about what you really want out of your life overall and out of your working life in particular. It can, of course, also give you a lump sum payoff and this can also be factored into the possibility of changes to your life that you may make. A sizeable redundancy payment combined with a cessation of work could be just the push you need to transform your life. At this point, nothing should be ruled out. You might move abroad, start a business, sort out your finances so that you never need worry about work again, or you may simply put the money in the bank, find a far less stressful job (but consequently lower paid) and live happily ever after knowing that you can afford not to have a job if the whim takes you.

This feeling of the opening up of lots of options is what you must concentrate on if you are to find your way through redundancy successfully. Quite apart from this attitude giving you more chances and choices, it will also ensure that you are able to maintain normal life without feeling the constant, miserable pressure of the fear of redundancy.

What next? Consider all your options

If you find yourself in a redundancy situation but you are sure that your performance in the job did not have any bearing on your selection, then it is quite likely that the industry you're in is going through a period of change and there may be a general downturn in that industry, so you should be sure to look at all your options. Do not automatically look for a job in the area with which you're familiar – the jobs there may be seriously depleted so your chances are lessened even before you start your search. You may have no choice but to try something new – and that's not a bad thing.

If you have been made redundant, you must look at all your options. This could mean looking at areas of work that you have never before considered, looking at different ways of working (two part-time jobs, for example, might replace your previous, full-time job) and checking out your chances of self-employment. You will need to be realistic, but maybe also creative about what you can do. You will need to look at your experience from an employer's point of view and really dig deep to find all the relevant bits of experience that you can offer. If you're in this situation, there will be more help as to how to do this in the final section in this chapter – the action plan – where you will consider your options.

One of your options is that of doing nothing. It is easy to assume that you must look for another job straight away and to throw yourself into job seeking to the detriment of everything else in your life. You apply for everything and anything that is in the least bit connected to your previous job – and get nowhere. At this point you must take some time to review exactly where you are and where you are going. Could you possibly arrange your finances and your life so that you can, in effect, happily consider the redundancy to mean early retirement? The chapters on money and on voluntary work later in this book may help you in this decision. The important thing is not to consider work to be the only thing in your life. It does not necessarily have to define you – you are more than just a job title. The 50s is an ideal time to review every area of your life and to see where the work/life balance needs to be addressed and it just might be that being made redundant will force you into this vital review. As with everything, it is necessary to keep an open mind and to give genuine consideration to every option.

Useful information

There is specialist help for people over 50 who find themselves in a redundancy situation. This includes:

- *New Deal 50 Plus* This is a voluntary programme for people over 50 who have been unemployed – and receiving benefits – for over six months. It offers a whole package of support to get you back into work, including a personal adviser.
- *The Prime Initiative* This again is a government initiative set up for the over 50s and will give you specialist advice on setting up your own business. They can also advise on finances and business development loans that may be available.
- *Job Centre Plus* This brings together employment advice and the benefits agency so can be invaluable if you're job hunting and struggling with your finances.
- *The Third Age Employment Network* This is a network of organisations whose aim is to ensure better opportunities for mature people. They are also leading campaigners on all matters related to age and employment. Their literature stresses the need to look after yourself if you're looking for work as maintaining your own well-being, motivation and confidence are important in any job search.
- *Age Concern* This organisation has a number of information sheets to help with finding work or setting up a business in later years.

Getting back into the workforce

The key to getting back into the workforce – if that is what you have decided is right for you – is to use everything you have. You need to make use of a variety of resources and advice and to present yourself so that you make sure that prospective employers appreciate just what you can do. Consult all the sources of information that you can find – including those specializing in advising the over 50s as shown above – and pick out the pieces of advice that are appropriate to you. Then find out just what is out there in terms of the job market. You can do this by:

- researching on the Internet where there are plenty of job search websites
- reading local (and national, if appropriate) newspapers
- visiting your local Jobcentre, because even if you think they will not have the sorts of vacancies for which you are looking, they do have copies of many relevant newspapers and other publications
- speaking to all your contacts, because many jobs are found by 'word of mouth'. If you can find out about a job and get your application in before it is advertised, you'll be ahead of the pack.

Your next task in your hunt for a suitable job is to prepare a CV that will present you in a way that will improve your chances. There are plenty of books available that will help you in preparing an eye-catching CV, but here are just a few points specifically aimed at older job seekers.

- Do not include your date of birth. Of course, any Human Resources department with even a half-awake staff could suss out your approximate age by a quick check on your job history but don't make it easy for any prospective employer to discard your CV before it has received at least a little attention.
- Put your skills and experience ay the beginning of your CV – where it can easily be seen – and relegate your work history to the end.
- Break down your skills and experience. Even if you've been with the same company most of your working life, you will still have wide-ranging experience that will be useful to other companies. Think about what you have done in your previous work that will be relevant to a new employer.

- Don't push the stereotypical older worker attributes. Your aim is to compete with younger applicants, so qualities such as enthusiasm, commitment to learning, adaptability and aptitude with new technology should be emphasised, rather than stability and maturity.

When you've found the jobs to apply for, prepare a CV that represents you well, your next job will be to win at the interview. Appearance is still important and as an older applicant you should look smart and up-to-date but don't end up as 'mutton dressed as lamb' – that will just draw attention to your age rather than playing it down. You will also need to be careful of how you approach your interviewer. If they are younger than you it is essential that you respect them rather than appear condescending. Make sure they appreciate that you can get on with all ages and types of people.

As an older applicant it is likely that you will have to try harder to get a new job than younger ones – it is an injustice but it is part of today's society so we have to deal with it. If you apply for enough jobs and have the right attitude, you will get back into the workplace.

Case study

After 15 years as an events manager for a major bank, Sonia was made redundant. With her generous redundancy package, she decided to set herself up as a property developer. She took a course on investing in property, read all she could lay her hands on about buying to let and signed up for a couple of evening classes on interior design and accounting for business. She asked around her friends and family for anyone with any relevant knowledge or contacts and also contacted local estate agents and letting agents to check out the market for rented properties in her area, checking out dozens of small properties that needed renovation. After all this research, she remained convinced that there was money to be made so she took the plunge and bought a small terraced house in need of a lot of work. She project-managed the renovation herself – enjoying it much more than her previous occupation – and even helped with some of the building work. When the builders moved out, she moved in to do the decorating and put the finishing touches to her first property development. She brought the project in on time and just over budget. As the local rentals market was stagnant at that point, rather than renting it out she sold the house at a substantial profit. Sonia immediately re-invested her money in two small properties and went on to develop dozens of properties in the next few years. She had turned her redundancy money into a real nest egg for her retirement and had found herself a new and immensely satisfying career.

Summary

Redundancy can be a traumatic experience for anyone, but for an older worker it is made especially difficult by ageist attitudes, making finding new employment more difficult. The whole experience can be made easier by adopting the right attitude. Thinking about it positively and being proactive will ensure that the stress levels caused will not get too high.

When you are made redundant, it is vital that you look at all your options. Consider alternative areas of employment, as your own industry may be in a period of decline, making it difficult to get a similar position. Consider self-employment, part-time employment or not working at all. Don't discard any idea until you've really examined the possibilities. There are specialist organisations to help you, following redundancy, and many of these have been listed above in this chapter.

If you decide you want to get back into the workplace, then you will have to do quite a bit of work including preparing a CV that pushes your age into the background, and finding job opportunities in all sorts of places, then applying for as many positions as possible to improve your chances of success.

Action plan: reviewing your options

Take a piece of paper and write down all the things that you could do with your life. This is, of course, a task with enormous scope and it will help to break this down into the following broad categories of the choices you may make in a redundancy situation in your 50s.

- Find a similar job to the one from which you have just been made redundant. This, as we said previously, can be difficult if your area is in a period of contraction and depression, but a bit of research locally will soon tell you whether this is the case and then you can see if finding a similar job is likely to be an option for you.

- Find a different type of job. A first step towards finding a new career is to define your ideal job. Can you imagine the surroundings, the hours you would be working, the people with whom you would be working, the type of organisation, the day-to-day routine? Think carefully about your options here and check out what types of vacancies in your chosen field are available locally.

- Retrain. It is not too late to acquire different skills in your 50s. You must be sure though, that these skills will be useful to you and that you do not spend too much time and money on courses without anything to show for them.

- Consider self-employment. Your first move should be to consider whether you are genuinely suited to self-employment (see Chapter 12 for more details about becoming self-employed). You should also develop your idea for a business on paper including preparing a written business plan and take care that you do not risk any more money than you can afford to lose in starting up a business. If you have a sizeable redundancy payment, put some of it away for 'rainy day money' and then invest only what you feel is absolutely necessary in your new business.

- Take early retirement. Obviously your finances will largely dictate whether this is an option or not and you should take expert advice on planning. Take care, too, that this option would really suit you. Many people feel that they just want to stop working and that doing nothing all day would be bliss, but some find that they don't have sufficient hobbies and interests. They then find that time weighs heavily. Consider what you would do with your time – travelling, hobbies, voluntary work, new activities? Will your finances stretch to all you would like to do in retirement or should you perhaps be considering part-time work?

12 self-employment

In this chapter you will learn:

- some things you need to know about self-employment
- how to check whether self-employment is for you
- how to make a business plan.

Self-employment in your 50s can be an ideal solution to problems such as redundancy, boredom with your current occupation or simply the need for a challenge. Whatever the reason for the change, becoming self-employed requires lots of careful thought, probably financial resources (at least enough to support you while you get the business off the ground, even if it doesn't require a lot of cash investment in property, materials or marketing), enormous personal resources (more about this later in this chapter), support from a partner, if you have one, and plenty of staying power. However, having said that the requirements are great, the rewards can be just as great. Of course, not every business makes pots of money for its founder, but the rewards can encompass things like personal satisfaction, freedom, a different lifestyle and not having a boss. Whatever you're looking for in becoming self-employed, it is almost always a good option for people with maturity, experience and resilience. I don't know anyone in the self-employed community who regrets their decision to work for themselves. Most say – and say it quite frequently – 'I wouldn't go back to working for someone else for anything'.

Why people start businesses in their 50s

Lots of the reasons why people start their own businesses in their 50s are the same as those that motivate people to become self-employed at any age. They want to take control of their working lives, or they have dreams of making a lot of money. However, there are particular reasons why, perhaps having had dreams of their own business for years while they have been bringing up a family or been busy earning enough money to pay the mortgage, they finally get around to making it a reality in their 50s. Sometimes there is an event, such as redundancy, that gives them the impetus and perhaps the financial wherewithal to go ahead. Sometimes they realise that their responsibilities have lessened sufficiently to allow them to take a chance on their dream of freedom from the 9 to 5 routine. Sometimes it can also be a feeling that life is passing them by that finally makes them make the move into self-employment. Or it can be a combination of all three of these reasons.

Although running your own business is never an easy ride, in your 50s you are often in a position to make the most of self-employment. By this stage in your life you will have plenty of experience. You will, hopefully, know what you want and be capable of being honest with yourself about your capabilities and the risks you are taking and will be prepared to take those risks without affecting your family too much. You will know how hard you have to work to earn a living but must accept that running your own business will not necessarily be easier – in fact, it is quite likely that you will end up working longer hours for your own business than for someone else's. In the next section we will look at the things you need to know about being self-employed.

Anita Roddick's story

One of the most well-known women to start a business is Anita Roddick. She founded her *Body Shop* empire, based on ethical beauty products, way back in 1976. Before this she had trained as a teacher, owned a restaurant and raised a family, so she is a prime example of someone with a varied career path. Her business made her a multi-millionairess and she has continued campaigning throughout her 50s and into her 60s for socially responsible business practices such as greener products and against sweatshop labour. She is widely quoted as saying 'I think the rich have to look after the poor' and has given a sizeable proportion of her fortune to causes close to her heart.

The reason she started her business was to support herself and her family but she did not lose sight of her ideals and used the business to help people less fortunate than herself.

Things you need to know about self-employment

The first thing you need to know about self-employment is why you are doing it. You need to examine your motivations in depth. If your reasons for becoming self-employed are not strong enough, you will not survive running your own business. When you start a business there will inevitably be problems and some very hard times. There may be times when there is very little money coming in and when you will not know where your next money is coming from – or when. There will be times when you're working very long hours for very little reward – apart from the satisfaction of running your own business. There is every chance that your new venture will take up more time than your old employment ever did and working for yourself might bring you a hard taskmaster for a boss – you! So you must be very sure that you know why you are doing it and what you want to get out of it. If your motivation is not strong enough it is quite likely that you will not make it through the difficult bits. You should therefore ask yourself lots of questions before you start a business. Establish your motives and examine the level of your commitment. Try asking yourself these questions:

- Why do I want to start my own business?
- What do I want to achieve?
- Am I doing this because I've been made redundant and don't know what else to do?
- Am I doing this to prove something to myself? Or to someone else?
- Am I prepared to risk the money I'm investing?
- How many hours per week do I expect to work in this business?
- Is my partner/family behind me in this venture?
- What will I do if this business fails?

Now, some of these questions – especially the last one – may seem negative. This is because you must force yourself to look at your motivations and at the new business from all angles. When you're considering setting up a business – perhaps something you've been thinking of for years – it is easy to get carried away with all the wonderful things that could be within your grasp. You could be looking forward to working in a field that has long fascinated you, or to taking things easier once you have no boss to answer to, or to building up an immensely profitable business, or simply to being the boss for a change. But wanting success is not enough. Of course, having bags of enthusiasm is vital when you're embarking on a life-changing new venture like this, but enthusiasm must be tempered with reality.

Is it for you?

In considering your motivation for becoming self-employed in the last section, you will have gone a long way towards discovering whether it is for you. So long as you have been honest with yourself and are not looking at the prospect of self-employment through rose-coloured spectacles, you will have considered whether you really can cope with the difficult times that will inevitably come as part of running a business. However, apart from the occasional hard times, there is also the day-to-day aspect of being self-employed that you should be sure you have appreciated and can cope with. Running your own business can be a lonely affair. It can also be difficult to keep going every day. You will have routine tasks to attend to and there will be no boss to demand that you do them. You must motivate yourself and make yourself stick at it even when you think half-an-hour sitting out in the garden would be preferable. So, being self-employed initially demands a set of skills and aptitudes that are not directly related to the area of business you have chosen – they apply to everyone who is in business.

- You must be self-disciplined. If you have doubts about your ability to resist daytime television when you should be doing your books or contacting your customers, then don't become self-employed. You need to be able to sit down and work, even when you know that it is a boring task that awaits you. There will be no-one else setting targets for you. The only person who will motivate you is you. Can you do that?

- You must like your own company. If you've decided to work from home, there will be many hours where you are on your own. If you really prefer to be surrounded by people then it is not for you. If you're still intent on becoming self-employed, look for something that will give you the opportunity to get out and meet the public. Of course, you will have sacrificed the freedom that comes with being self-employed and working from home but hard choices do have to be made and it is more important to create a business that is right for you than merely to make life easy for yourself.

- You must trust your own judgement. You will be making the decisions. We have all criticized the decisions made by former bosses and felt we could do better but it is easier to criticise than it is to take all the responsibility yourself. Can you make decisions easily or do you dither and worry about what you should do?

- You will need plenty of self-confidence. When things go wrong – as they will, sometimes – you must have the self-confidence and the resilience to pick yourself up, shrug your shoulders and get on with putting things right.

What you really need to do in asking yourself the question 'Is it for me?' is make sure that you are temperamentally suited to self-employment. Can you cope when disaster strikes – because whatever happens, it will be your problem – and, just as importantly, can you cope if you have great success? Of course, we'll all answer 'Yes! Give me the money!' to that last question, but do you really have the discipline to carry on answering the phone to impatient customers or keep up with the weekly tasks of doing the books or cleaning the office when you know that you've hit the jackpot? Or are you the type to shut up shop for a week so that you've got time for a spot of serious retail therapy? The point here is that no matter what happens, good or bad, a business has to carry on. You will be committed to keeping it going. If you don't, your investment and all your marketing efforts will have been wasted because unreliability is death to a business. Having said that, it is perfectly possible to set up a business that fits in with your life so that you won't be tied to it 24 hours a day, seven days a week. A young mother I know has set up a holistic therapy centre in her dining room and she only commits to opening three days a week and will not book clients in for treatments later than 2.30 p.m. because she wants to be there to collect her children from school. Despite the restrictions she puts on it, she has a good, profitable business. It does not dictate to her and does not stop her living her life as she wants to live it. However, it is also possible to set up a business that demands every minute of your time, so if all you want is a part-time occupation with part-time commitment, take care what sort of business you set up and the rules you set for it. Don't make promises that you can't keep.

Above all, you must decide if you're really suited to being your own boss. As bad as previous bosses have been, your boss when you work for yourself can be worse. You could be unforgiving of yourself, a hard taskmaster and inconsistent. Or you could be lazy and hardly ever put in a full day at work. Either way, you will have a difficult boss.

What sort of business?

Many people in their 50s who have perhaps taken early retirement will not want to stop work completely but are definite that they don't want to work for anyone else for the rest of their active life. They want to work for themselves. In this case they may not have anything specific that they know they want to do as a business but maybe have a few vague ideas of what their strengths are and what they might like to do that will earn a bit of money. Finding ideas in this situation is not a problem; there are lots and lots of things that can be developed into a business. Even if you only want to go into business in a small way, perhaps only devoting part-time hours to it and with no big ambitions to earn a fortune, you must still follow a few important rules of becoming self-employed at this stage in your life:

- Don't risk your entire financial future on a business. Be very sure that you can afford to risk the money that you calculate it will take to start your business. At this stage in your life, retirement, in financial terms at least, may not be very far away so you must make financial provision for this.
- Draw up a sound business plan. This is essential no matter how small the business you are planning may be. All the major banks have forms and software that can help you with drawing up a business plan and there is plenty of information online. You need to know what your goals are from a financial point of view, how much money will be going out and also when you can expect money to start coming in, so do not be tempted to skip this part of your preparations. When you've got a plan together, take it to your bank or an accountant for their professional opinion.
- Consider all your options. You do not have to carry on in the same field in which you have worked all your life. You will, if you examine yourself closely, have plenty of other knowledge and experience that can be used in different areas. If you really want to 'stick with what you know' then check out the possibilities for passing on your knowledge as a consultant or maybe a part-time lecturer.

Even with these provisos, you will still be left with plenty of choices. Do you want to work from home, for instance? Or do you want to go further afield? Have you considered a franchise? All of these ideas will give you lots of options.

Working from home can offer many advantages including great flexibility, low risk (you're not paying for business premises) and great satisfaction that you have created a job for yourself and are completely your own boss – all things that are very attractive to someone in their 50s who wants to go into business in a small way. Choices could include, for example, bookkeeping or book writing, toy making or typing, translating or music teaching, fancy dress hire or floristry – the list is endless. To make a decision here you will need to list all the things that you already know or could learn about (maybe you've always been artistic and could take classes in floristry, for example, or you're already fluent in a foreign language) and then brainstorm business ideas based on what's on your list. Also include your strengths. You might not consider reliability or liking animals to be things that you could make a business out of but if these apply to you, put them down. You could start a dog-walking or animal-sitting business.

If you want to get out of the house – even if it's for a limited number of hours every week, there are plenty of choices here too. You could be a lorry driver or a consultant passing on your knowledge to local businesses. You could become a caterer or a cleaner. You could deliver pizzas or be a house sitter. All of these options will get you out of the house and into a self-employed, earning situation. They won't all bring you into contact with many people – a house sitter will be alone most of the time, for example, although this is something you could do as a couple and as a pizza delivery person you won't get much chance to have meaningful conversations with people, so if social contact is important to you these two choices won't be ideal. They won't bring you a lot of money either, so consider all your options carefully.

If it appeals to you, you should check out the options for a franchised business. There is plenty of information available on the Internet or in the library and Chambers of Commerce will usually have advice sections for business that include details of many franchises. There are also regular Franchise Fairs held in many major cities where you could take a general look around at what's available and decide if it's for you. Options range from starting one of the large takeaway food outlets to a lawn care service and everything you could think of in between. The obvious advantage is that franchises offer a tried and tested business idea with plenty of support and advice already in place, but franchises vary tremendously. Some can be started for an outlay of a few thousand pounds while others involve investments of hundreds of thousands. Some have very slick, well-tested systems in place while others are in their very early days. Some could earn you lots of money while others could cost you everything you own. So take care and take advice.

Summary

In this chapter we've looked at what you should do to assess your suitability for self-employment and at the things you should consider if you do decide to become self-employed.

We looked at the qualities you need to be able to successfully start your own business and, apart from a great business idea and lots of the skills associated with running a business, we saw that these included self-discipline, feeling comfortable working independently, plenty of self-confidence and the ability to make decisions.

There are lots of choices to be made before you get your business up and running and this chapter aimed to help you with those choices.

Action plan: create a business plan

Anyone seriously thinking about setting up in business should create a business plan – even before going to professionals for advice. This will serve two purposes.

- It will clarify your thoughts and let you see for yourself if your idea is viable. You will need to do plenty of research to get to the point where you can write your business plan, finding out things like what you will be able to charge for your proposed product or service, who will be your customers and how you will get them to buy. A good business plan will serve the purpose of a map – it will help you to see where you are going and how you are going to get there.
- It will be a useful document if you need to approach anyone for a loan or when you ask professionals for advice.

Even if your idea is just a rough one at the moment, try to create a business plan following the suggested headings below:

What's your idea?

This is just a short explanation of what you propose to do. State the nature of your business, where it will be based and how it will make money.

What's your mission?

Sometimes the act of writing a mission statement can focus the mind. It will make you see what you are aiming at and why. Think about the objectives your business will have – things such as when you expect to go into profit, when you expect to be at your peak of profitability, how many customers you will need or how many items you will need to sell to achieve your aims. Then try to encapsulate your aims and what you will offer the marketplace in a short, motivating sentence or two. Someone planning a dog-walking business might say something like 'I will provide a reliable, friendly service in all weathers and aim to have five regular customers by the end of the second month in business'.

Your marketing plan

What is the size of your potential market? Who are your competitors? How did you find out these things? How will you make your business and its benefits known to your market? Put all these things into this section so that you are clear about where you will direct your sales and marketing efforts. Obviously, at this stage you will need to estimate many of the items that go into your marketing plan – the number of customers you expect, your business costs and so on – but base these estimates on some solid information that you have collected in your research. To go back to the dog-walking business as an example, make sure that you have approached as many dog owners as possible and recorded how many of them – percentage-wise – would be prepared to use such a service if it was offered to them and how much they might be prepared to pay. You could then include in your plan that 10 per cent of local dog owners out of an estimated 200 within the area you plan to cover (you'll have to research this figure, perhaps by approaching a local vet or animal sanctuary for their estimates or simply counting the number of different dogs being walked in spots popular with dog owners in your area) would be prepared to pay £X per hour for your service. Think, too, about extra services you might offer – taking animals to the vet, grooming, etc. and put this into your plan for the future development of your business.

Will it make money?

Next you will need to show that your idea is a money-maker. To do this you must prepare a profit-and-loss account to cover the first year of your business. The format for a profit-and-loss account is usually as follows:

Total sales
Less purchases
= Gross profit
Less overheads such as
  Premises costs (rent, rates)
  Heat, light, power, water
  Staff costs (wages, NI Contributions)
  Sales, Marketing and advertising costs
  Telephone
  Vehicle(s)

Insurance
Professional charges (accountant etc.)
Repairs
Insurance etc.
Postage
= Operating profit

Where will the money come from?

Are you going to invest your life savings? And, if so, can you afford to lose what you are investing? Or will you need to borrow from a bank? Or from friends and family? If you're borrowing money, you will need to show in your business plan exactly how you will pay this money back. The bank will be particularly keen to know this.

Your plan will also need to show how this money will be spent. Do you need it to buy special equipment or stock to sell? Or is it for you to live on until the business becomes profitable?

Your cash flow

This is a more complicated exercise and relies on your estimates of income and expenditure. It shows what money you expect to be coming into and going out of your business month by month and will show whether or not your business can survive its first year. Poor cash flow is probably one of the most common reasons for a business to fail. It is possible for a business to be essentially profitable but if the money coming in does not match or exceed the money going out for a period of time, then a business can quickly get into difficulties. For these reasons it is particularly important to do this exercise and to do it carefully. Use the grid on page 132 to help.

Estimated income and expenditure for the first year of the business

	Jan	Feb	Mar	Apr	May	Jun	Jul	Aug	Sep	Oct	Nov	Dec	Total
Income													
Sales													
Loans													
Capital													
Total Income													
Outgoings													
Purchases													
Wages, national insurance													
Drawings													
Rent, rates													
Gas, water, electricity,													
Telephone													
Postage													
Loan repayments													
Accountant													
Travel costs													
Other expenses													
Total outgoings													

When you've filled this in as accurately as you can at this stage, you will need to compare the total planned income and outgoings on a monthly basis as well as over the complete year. Are there any trouble spots? If there are months where it is obvious that your business will not be able to pay its way, you will need to take corrective action.

When your business is up and running, this document is just as important in ensuring the health of your business. Keep the figures in the cash flow statement up to date and try to look ahead when using it, then your business will have a much greater chance of success.

This has been only a very brief exercise aimed at helping you to focus on your business idea and to get together the basics of a business plan. This might be sufficient for your purposes if you are starting a small, home-based business with very low start-up costs that will mean you are not taking many risks. If, however, you will need to borrow money to put your business idea into action or will be taking an appreciable risk with your own capital, then you will need to do lots more research and to prepare a more detailed plan to ensure the viability of your idea. There are plenty of books on the market that will help in the preparation of a detailed business plan and also with the start-up phase of a business.

13

money

In this chapter you will learn:
- how to check how much money you really need
- how to start some serious financial planning
- how to set a budget.

Money is a very emotive issue. We all have different attitudes towards it and most of us think we haven't got enough of it. And it doesn't get easier as you get older. There are very few people of any age who don't worry about money at all. When you're in your 20s and 30s, establishing yourself on the property ladder and coping with the demands of a young family will mean that you worry about money extremely frequently. When you're in your 40s and 50s, children at university will cause concern. By the time you're into your 50s you will be not only worrying about current concerns – such as your offspring, home maintenance and job security – but the future will loom large in your thoughts too. It is now, as you turn 50, that you will need to seriously consider your pension provision – if you haven't already.

In recent years there has been a great loss of confidence in the financial industry and the whole question of pension provision has become blurred and frightening. A decade or so ago it was accepted that we paid into a company pension, stayed in the job for 20 or 30 years and at the end of our working lives, came out with a reasonable company pension which, added to our state entitlement, would mean that we had a degree of security in our old age. That simplicity and security has gone. With the failure of several high-profile company schemes, endowment mis-selling and problems with the stock market at the end of the twentieth and beginning of the twenty-first centuries, many people are struggling to know what to do to make sure that they have adequate financial resources in old age. One thing that has not changed, however, during all this uncertainty, is that if we make no provision for our own financial security in old age, then we will be destined to a retirement marred by poverty. The state provision is unlikely ever to be totally sufficient for all our needs.

How much do you really need?

Although there is no doubt that we must save and invest for our retirements, many people make the mistake of thinking that we will need the same monthly income at 70 as we do at 50. Do you have a mortgage now? Will you still be paying it at 70? Do you have loans or credit card bills? Think about how your circumstances may change in the next ten or 20 years and you may be pleasantly surprised by the amount you will actually need to live on. Consider these changes that may happen as you retire:

• your mortgage may be paid off
• debts related to cars or other large items may be paid off

- your children will, hopefully, have become independent
- if you and your partner drive two large cars now, maybe you will only need one when you no longer have to go to work or you will be able to trade down to smaller, less expensive models
- you may move to a smaller home, resulting in smaller household bills and also some capital being freed up
- you will probably eat less as you become less active and you will not have to buy lunch at work every day
- you will no longer need smart suits to wear to work every day – your weekend wardrobe will become what you wear all the time when you no longer work
- transport costs should decrease
- you will be able to take advantage of the reductions that are available to old age pensioners – bus passes, discounts on certain days at the hairdressers, at the cinema, at a variety of tourist attractions and even at DIY stores.

Taking these positive points into account, you will need to develop a detailed budget as you approach retirement. Make sure that you do not cut it too close to the bone – leave a margin for error to allow for inflation, unforeseen expenditure and emergencies. For now, unless your retirement is imminent, all you can do is estimate your needs and tailor your savings and investments to suit.

Pensions and planning

Your first step in planning your financial affairs for retirement is to accurately predict just how much income you are going to have. You can get a forecast of how much your state pension will be by writing to the Department of Social Security (details at back of this book) and for your occupational and private pensions by contacting your pension provider(s). For women in particular, there may be shortfalls in your contribution record (because of time taken out of the workforce for family responsibilities, etc.) and now is the time to find out about the shortfall and decide whether it will be worth your while to make payments to make it up so that you can get the maximum state retirement pension. Consider also whether you will have any endowments or other policies maturing around your retirement time and gather details of the expected payouts from these. You should also add in any income you can expect to receive from savings and investments, but these will, of course, be largely dependent on the rate of interest during your retirement so it is impossible to be 100 per cent accurate in your forecasts here.

Having gathered all your predictions of income and expenditure, you are in a position to move on to the next step – that of assessing the investment and savings necessary to secure your old age.

Savings, insurance, shares and inheritance

Any serious attempt at financial planning for your retirement is better done with input from a specialist financial adviser. However, you certainly can – and should – gather all your figures and details together before your appointment with him or her.

Your 50s is an ideal time to get your financial affairs in order – if you haven't done so already. During the decade from 50 to 60 there will probably be a variety of financial changes taking place. Your family responsibilities will probably lessen (although you may have to take on responsibilities for your parents' generation – more about this in Chapter 7), your income from employment will probably have reached its peak, your mortgage will probably come to an end and you will start to see a clear path to retirement. These changes will, in the main, make your financial affairs more straightforward and predictable. You will still, however, have to put in quite a bit of effort if you want to be organised. Do you know, for example, what rate of interest is currently being paid on any ISAs or savings accounts or the current price for any shares that you own?

Set aside an hour or two to get all your financial details together. If you haven't already done so, make proper files to keep savings and investment details together so that when statements are received they can be checked and filed away without fuss and you will know just where you can lay your hands on them when you're doing your tax return or the next time you're checking your finances.

A word here about people who leave all this sort of thing to their partners (and men do this as well as women) – this is a lazy approach and it's dangerous. If you don't understand and keep up to date with your financial details, how can you plan your future? And what if your partner – for whatever reason – was no longer around? Resolve right now to remedy this situation. The two things you need to know about are income and expenditure. Where does all your money come from and where does it go? Make simple, straightforward lists of everything that comes in – salaries, interest on savings and investments, dividends, pensions maybe and so on. Then make another list of everything you spend. Think about this on a weekly, monthly and yearly basis. If you just think about monthly outgoings you may miss the annual bills that come in such as insurance or council tax and if you don't look at weekly expenditure you may ignore the small items such as the coffees you buy at work or sweets, magazines and newspapers that you pay cash for.

Right, you're ready to give your financial affairs an overhaul. Having got all the relevant paperwork together, it's a good idea to start lists of all your savings and investments. These can, of course, simply be handwritten lists, but if you have a computer it's an easy job to keep a list on there that can be updated once or twice a year, depending on how much and how often your savings circumstances change. Note on this list important dates such as when bonds mature, when dividends are due and what rate of interest each savings account is currently paying. This is all information that a financial adviser will find invaluable and it may well save you – and him or her – a lot of time and also enable you to make better decisions.

When you've summarized your income, savings and investments in this way and looked at your expenditure, you can see clearly where your money comes from and, just as importantly, where it goes to. You will be able to see if you will have sufficient income in retirement and, with the help of your financial adviser, will be able to revise your arrangements. At this point it is useful to remember that pensions are simply a tax wrapper. They are the most tax efficient way of saving long term for your retirement – but they are not the only way. When you've reached your 50s, you may feel that there is not much time left in your working life to make further pension provision – that depends mainly upon your planned retirement age – but there are other ways to make savings without paying tax on the interest or tying up your money for the years leading up to your retirement. Using your ISA allowances at this stage is a must and your financial adviser will be able to give you full details of the current rules.

There are several changes you can make for yourself if they are needed, before you see an expert.

- Now that you know where your savings are and what rate of interest each account is paying, move any amounts, however small, out of accounts that are paying low rates of interest into ones that pay a higher rate. The Internet is a useful resource for finding the accounts offering the best rates of interest and some web-based accounts have slightly better rates of interest than those that are operated via premises on the high street.

- Consider your plans for any shares that you hold. How have they performed over the time that you have held them? Why are you holding them? Over the long term shares will almost certainly out-perform other forms of investment but you should not hold on to them blindly – they need to pay their way in your savings and investment portfolio like any other item.

- If you have bonds that are due to mature, consider where you will put the money at that time. Do not just blindly let them be 'rolled over' into an alternative account or bond with the same provider. Be proactive and seek out a better deal for yourself.

- Check whether you've got the best possible deal on your mortgage. Even at this stage when your mortgage may be coming up to its last year or two, there are still deals to be had. Check with your current provider first, as they will often be prepared to better your interest rate in order to keep your custom. Check out rates available on the Internet and on the High Street too.

- Review your insurance policies and decide whether they are still appropriate for your current and future situations. If you have Income Protection Insurance, for example, but have changed your employment status to self-employed since you took out the policy, then it probably would not pay out. Check it out. Maybe you have a policy for your dependents – but no longer have any dependents. It is important to realise that all financial products must be reviewed regularly and insurances are just one more financial product in your portfolio.

- Is inheritance tax likely to be a problem for you? To assess your individual situation you will need to consult an expert. There are lots of factors to consider such as the value of all your assets including your home and any other property you own, your savings and investments and also to whom you intend to leave all these assets in the event of your death. Currently assets can be left to a spouse free of inheritance tax but the problem crops up when large amounts of assets are being left to offspring. Avoiding paying too much tax is not easy, but there are things that you can do to prepare yourself, so make use of a competent adviser, especially if you currently have assets in excess of the current inheritance tax nil rate band.

Save or spend? – A compromise

Whether you save like crazy for the last decade or so of your working life in a desperate, last ditch attempt to secure your old age or ignore the future and live for the present, spending everything you earn, will depend largely on your personality. It will, of course, also depend to some extent on what your review of your finances revealed, but most people will not change drastically at this stage in their lives no matter what provision they have made – or not made – for their retirement.

A useful compromise is to do a bit of both saving and spending. Save, yes, but don't do it to the detriment of your quality of life. It is important to make the most of this very important decade of your life. Take adventurous holidays now while you're still able. Keep your self-esteem high and your enjoyment of life at a peak by doing whatever is necessary. This might mean pampering yourself with spa treatments or buying new clothes. Whatever it takes to make you enjoy your 50s and is, of course, within your means, is exactly what you should be doing. And if there is something that you've always wanted to do – whether it be climbing a mountain, going on a luxury cruise, backpacking around Europe or learning a foreign language – then now is definitely the time to do it. While you just might reach 80 and regret the fact that you don't have a few more hundred pounds in the bank, you are far more likely to find yourself sitting in your chair at 80 wishing that you'd taken up all your opportunities when you were able.

The best way to make your decision about saving or spending is to work out your budget – see the action plan at the end of this chapter – including a percentage of your total income for savings and investment (and don't forget that any existing occupational pension scheme that you're currently paying into direct from your salary counts as savings), then add in an amount for fulfilling your dreams. This is not frivolous, it's what you must do if your aim is to enjoy your life – and isn't that everybody's aim?

Summary

In this chapter you've:

- looked carefully at your finances
- prepared yourself for a visit to your financial adviser for a serious overhaul of your retirement planning
- looked at a few ways of ensuring your savings are on the right track to providing a comfortable retirement
- considered planning for inheritance tax – a job for the experts
- assessed whether you should be saving or spending – or a bit of both.

Action plan: setting a budget

If you can keep track of your income and outgoings – even if you have never done this in a formal way before – you will have a very good chance of being in control of them. Set up a system now and it will stand you in good stead for when finances inevitably become more limited when you retire.

First, you must write down every single source of income you have. Don't forget to include overtime, commission or bonuses from your main employment, interest and dividends from every savings or investment account you have, any spare-time earnings you have and any perks of your job such as a car or meal vouchers. Total all these items for the year then divide by 52 to arrive at your average weekly income.

Second, you have to list all your outgoings. Try to work it out on a weekly basis as this will enable you to see more easily exactly where your money goes. Most people will have a monthly income at this stage in their lives but it is too easy to forget smaller items of expenditure over a period of a month whereas what you spend on a weekly basis will be more obvious. For instance, your main food shopping is probably done weekly, your newspaper bill will be sent every week and there will be numerous small items such as birthday cards, dry cleaning and postage that you can easily keep track of every week. Everything else – all your monthly bills for insurance or your quarterly bills for utilities such as electricity, gas and telephone costs – can be worked out annually and then divided by 52 to arrive at an average weekly amount. Don't forget to include those larger items of expenditure that are only occasional such as holidays and Christmas or birthday gifts for family and friends during the course of a year. Add in a realistic estimate of what you will spend on clothes in a year, too.

Your next step, of course, is to compare the totals that you have arrived at. Hopefully, your income will exceed your outgoings by an appreciable amount. If it doesn't then you will have some extra work to do. Examine your outgoings and save money wherever you can. Maybe you could cut down on the amount you spend on lunches at work by making your own sandwiches or cancel the daily newspaper delivery – you probably only read the weekend ones thoroughly anyway. You should also check your income at this point to see if there is anything you can do to maximize it but it is almost always easier to reduce your expenditure.

Assuming that your income and expenditure are not too far apart, you will now be in a position to balance this budget on a weekly basis. To do this, you will need to take the third step – keeping a weekly expenditure log. This is simply writing down everything you spend. This may well be an illuminating experience and will almost certainly result in you resolving to be a bit more careful. When you realise that those daily coffees with fancy names are costing an appreciable percentage of your weekly budget, maybe you'll start to keep them for a treat rather than a daily must-have. At the end of each week, you'll be able to see from this budget whether you're living within your means and, hopefully, you'll be able to see some surplus income that can be saved or invested.

giving something back

In this chapter you will learn:

- some reasons for volunteering
- how to research volunteering opportunities
- how to find your niche.

There are lots of reasons why people take up voluntary work when they retire. Some realise that voluntary work is something that will bring them into contact with people – the social side of working – without the commitment to turning up every day or working full days. It can be a chance to be in a working environment again but there is often no real responsibility attached to voluntary work. You can work with a greater degree of freedom and control than you may have been used to having in a conventional work situation. Many see it as a chance, now that they do not have to go out to work every day, to do something for others – to give something back. Here again, the reasons for wanting to do it are varied – lots of voluntary workers choose a cause that is close to their hearts such as the well-known charities like Oxfam or the NSPCC and find it easy to work on that charity's behalf, feeling grateful that they are not in need of the charity's services, while others work for a charity that has helped them or their family such as a cancer or heart disease research organisation or a local hospice. Still others join a political organisation such as one of the major parties or an environmental charity. Whatever your choice of voluntary work – it will be rewarding and is unlikely to be something that you will regret. It will enrich your life in lots of ways while giving you an outlet for your energy and commitment.

Why volunteering is important

Voluntary work can be rewarding in many ways but one of the most important changes it can make to a retired person's life is the feeling it gives of making a useful contribution to society. When you leave work and stop earning a salary, it is common to feel a bit 'cast adrift' and as though your useful life is over. The same feeling can come along and hit you when children leave home and you're left behind at home with a reduced workload. Both of these events are likely to happen – or at least hove into view – during your 50s and voluntary work can be the ideal way of combating the negative feelings that may accompany these life changes.

Of course, the main reason for volunteering is to make a difference. You want to help others and to use your time for the good of others who may not have your advantages. You may be blessed with a secure financial situation, good health and an ability to help yourself through life but at the same time you are very much aware that others do not have all these things. If you can help one person, or one animal or your favourite cause to improve their situation then you will derive a great deal of satisfaction from volunteering. If you have a choice between sitting at home and having another cup of coffee with your morning newspaper or getting out into your community and making a difference, then there is no contest. You will gain far more from volunteering than almost any other activity you could name. There have even been studies that suggest that people who spend just one day a week doing some form of voluntary work can increase their expected life span by up to two years, so there must be some benefit to be had – for yourself as well as others.

Voluntary work can also be very enjoyable in that it is so different from your regular occupation and will not actually feel like work. There will be much less pressure regarding hours – although see the next section about saying 'no' – and about the level of work you undertake. In most cases, you will set the limits. If you only want to do a few hours a week or more prolonged bursts of work and then nothing for a while, the choice is yours. You are free to lead a life of your own, but every single hour that you do give to your chosen cause will be truly appreciated. Although you will not receive a pay packet for any work you do on a voluntary basis, of course, you will feel that you have been rewarded in many other ways.

Saying 'no'

Having said that you usually set the limits of your involvement with your voluntary work, it is easily conceivable that you will be asked to do more if there is a shortage of volunteers in your area. The thing to remember is that this work is just what it says it is – voluntary. The choice is yours and you must make sure that you do not agree to do more work than you really want to do. If you are asked to do more and you would rather be doing something else or have another commitment, say so. You do not even have to give reasons, a simple 'No, I'm sorry, I can't' will suffice. Any time that you can give will be appreciated and it is important that you do not feel under pressure and that you enjoy your involvement. After all, your paid employment is (or was) enough of a commitment and you do not want to add resentment to your life at this stage. Make sure that you know exactly what you are committing yourself to and that the hours you agree to are ones that will fit around your other commitments and activities.

Researching opportunities in your community

When you start to look for voluntary work that you can do in your local area, you will be astounded by the choice that is out there. There are a number of websites (see the section on useful organisations and websites at the back of this book for details) that will be able to give you plenty of contacts to start you off in your search for the perfect opportunity for you. Choosing what you want to get involved in will probably prove more difficult than finding someone who is looking for volunteers. Some websites even have the facility for you to enter your postcode and then you are given specific opportunities that are currently available very close to your home.

The variety of voluntary work that you can choose from is enormous. You could do anything from working in a charity shop on your high street to helping out in a scheme for disadvantaged children. You might want to get involved with something connected with a charity that is of particular importance to you. For instance, you may have witnessed the wonderful service offered by your local hospice or seen how valued the ladies working the snack trolley at your local hospital are. Or you may already have a connection to a charitable cause such as the RNIB or RNLI. Or you may want to get involved with a more political cause so that you can change the world around you. If you want to 'do your bit' for an environmental cause or help a campaign against world poverty then volunteering could be for you and you should contact your nearest branch of the appropriate organisation.

Before you volunteer, and to help you make the right choice for you, you should ask yourself a number of questions:

- How much time do I really want to spend on this? It is a good idea to start cautiously as it is often easier to step up your commitment rather than scale it back.
- When do I have free time? Weekends, evenings or daytimes during the week? This may determine exactly what you can get involved in. If you want to help on the administration side of a large charity, then you will probably need to be free on weekdays but if you want to help out at a local animal shelter, then they will probably be glad of some help at any time but particularly in the evenings or at weekends.

- What special interests would I like to pursue? What are my particular passions? You may wish to get involved in the arts, or local heritage, or an animal charity, for example.
- Do I have special skills and experience that could be useful as a volunteer? If you have marketing skills you may be welcomed by a wide variety of organisations as a voluntary worker and with information technology skills you may need to find a charity specifically working in this area, with young people perhaps.
- Is there a special charity or organisation with which I have a connection? As we said earlier, you may feel you want to give something back to a local hospice or you may want to get involved with a charity such as Cancer Research or a Special School that has helped a member of your family.
- Where do I want to work? This is an important factor as it may dictate which charities and organisations you can consider. If you don't want to – or can't – drive then there is little point in considering work 50 miles away on a regular basis. This is where the websites that can help you search for local organisations will come in handy. Alternatively, you may want to get out and about, so looking for volunteer opportunities that involve a bit of travelling will be appropriate. You may even want more of a challenge and be happy to spend time away from home. If so, volunteering for overseas work may be for you.
- For what sort of organisation do I want to work? Am I looking for a friendly environment working with other volunteers or members of the organisation's staff or maybe I would prefer working one-to-one with someone? Must it be a charitable organisation or would I be just as happy working, on a voluntary basis, in a commercial concern?
- With whom do I want to work? Do I want to put my efforts into helping disadvantaged young people, for instance, or would I be happier with older people?
- Do I want to get some practical training or experience? Or is this just for fun (apart from 'giving something back', of course)? Consider what experience you would like to get – maybe mentoring would appeal to you or helping out behind-the-scenes at a local theatre.

As you can see, there are a lot of things to consider when you are about to get involved in voluntary work and it does help to have fully understood your motivations and likes and dislikes before you start. When you start your search in earnest, you will probably be amazed by the volume and variety of opportunities that exist. A good way to start your search is to browse on the Internet – see the websites mentioned at the end of this book – where you will see how far volunteering can take you.

Of course, if you're keen to put something right but you can't find any evidence of anyone else doing anything about a problem, you could start your own 'good cause'. Many people in their 50s are at the heart of local campaigns to solve all sorts of problems. If there is a landfill site planned near your home or something else that you feel passionately about, you could start a campaign against it, enlisting help from people who feel almost as passionately about the subject as you do but who had not been proactive enough to get going or who needed some direction from someone like you. If you want to do something about the crowds of youths hanging around the streets, you could be the one to start some sort of activity or meeting place for them. Whatever the problem, if you feel strongly enough about it, you can also do something about it. This could give you a whole new view on life and will bring you into contact with lots of different people from all walks of life.

Janet's story

Janet, a local newsagent, had fumed for years about the amount of litter discarded on the streets and green areas of the pretty little town she lived in. She would go out of her shop at the end of every day, armed with her rubber gloves and a black plastic bin bag and collect all the cigarette packets, drinks cans, crisp packets and other assorted litter. She knew that if she didn't do it, no one would. In the alleyway down the side of her shop – a particularly popular area with schoolchildren who would drop their litter there – she put up a Day-Glo orange sign saying 'Make Janet happy – use the bin!' This improved things for a while but, of course, did nothing about other untidy areas of the town. She got so mad about it that she contacted the local council. They sent round an officer who accompanied Janet around the area as she told him 'We need a bin here – and here – and here…' She got her point across and got her bins. Next she put a letter in the local paper and through this made contact with the lady who was to become secretary of the group that was to be called 'The Clean Team'. A few people who had admired Janet's efforts from afar joined in and they held a meeting in her dining room. They sent letters to local schools, supermarkets, churches, traders – anyone they could think of who might have some influence. Next, the group's official inaugural meeting attracted 39 people. Janet then organised her first litter pick, supplying a few bin bags, gloves and plastic aprons and they set to their task early on a cold, drizzly Saturday morning. People came along the street and, while some gave funny looks and passed by, many were more curious and asked what was going on. At the end of three hours the little band of litter pickers had ten sacks of rubbish and a feeling of satisfaction that made them go home with smiles on their faces.

Now, three years later, Janet is part of a team of 130 people who regularly take part in litter picks, gets regular press coverage of her campaign and has won a civic award in recognition of her efforts. She also has an enormous feeling of achievement and real pride in her town. The difference she has made is obvious. It only takes one person with the passion to do something to bring about a major change.

Summary

Getting involved in voluntary work can have far-reaching, important effects. It can not only help the charity or organisation for which you work but can give you a new lease of life in your 50s. It can provide a sense of purpose where perhaps you had lost direction after retiring or the children leaving home; it can open up a whole new world for you in terms of the people with whom you are in contact and the view of life that you are able to see on a daily basis; it can give you a change of direction and pace; it can even lengthen your life. Whatever you hope to get out of volunteering it is important to choose the work you do and to give plenty of thought to what you are prepared to put in. If the hours that you give to a good cause escalate to more than you feel comfortable with, volunteering will soon come to feel as much of a chore as working for your living can do. So, it is essential to do your research and be sure that you give just what you want to give.

Action plan: Finding your niche

Sit down and think seriously about who you want to help – and why. The reasons why we undertake voluntary work vary from person to person and before you are able to find something that is right for you, you need to understand your motives.

Most people decide to help a charity or organisation that is close to their heart for some reason and there will be no decision to be made about for whom you're going to do some voluntary work. If your path is not so clear it can be a good move to list a few charities whose work you admire or think are particularly relevant to you and then you will be able to research the opportunities that exist in the organisations on your list.

Next you need to review your skills. What can you offer an organisation and what would you enjoy doing? If you would be bored by doing administrative work, then there would be little point in volunteering for that sort of opportunity. But if you think that getting out and about brandishing a collection tin is for you, then you will be drawn to that.

Your next step is to research what is on offer in the organisations or areas you've chosen. The Internet can be useful here (see the list at the end of this book) or you could simply approach the organisations upon which you've decided. Most charities have someone who will coordinate volunteer activity and will be glad to hear from willing workers.

Voluntary work should be rewarding so choose carefully what you commit yourself to. Sometimes, even routine tasks can be interesting so don't rule those out but if you go against your own desires and skills, you will probably not keep up the effort long-term, so it is better for everyone concerned for you to be selective about the sort of tasks with which you get involved. You will get the satisfaction of helping and being interested and the charity or other organisation will gain a regular and useful volunteer.

15

where to next?

In this chapter you will learn:
- how to pull your plan for the next decade together
- how to complete a life chart
- which area of your life you need to concentrate on.

We've looked at all the different areas of your life and you will hopefully, by now, have seen that life – even in your 50s! – is well worth living. You will have seen that your life may not be perfect, but it has plenty to offer. You are not at the end of your life – you're in the middle – and it is up to you to make the most of your future. Just what your future holds is up to you. This book may have prompted you to think about issues such as how fit you are and how healthy your diet is, when – or if – you should retire, how you could change your working life, how you deal with the older and younger generations and how you spend your spare time. All of these things will make up your future and if there are areas of dissatisfaction then that is where you must go next.

Pulling your plan together

You will now need to put together a plan that addresses these areas of dissatisfaction and to allocate some time and perhaps other resources to solving the problems that you have uncovered. Your aim is to make the best of your life, taking into account all the benefits and drawbacks that come with mid-life. Being in your 50s does not mean that you must put up with what you've got, it just means that you must make the effort now to improve things so that you will have plenty of time left to enjoy the fruits of your labours. In order to do this you need a plan. This can only be pulled together when you fully appreciate your current situation and where improvements are necessary. When you get to this stage, and if you've worked your way through the book, you're nearly there (it just needs a little thought to bring things together). You are ready to take action. It is essential that you prioritize your actions, so we'll look at that in the next section.

On which area will you concentrate?

In this book we've looked at many areas of your life – your work, your leisure, your family, your commitments and responsibilities – and all of them will be important to you. However, having examined each of these areas as you've gone through the chapters, it is probably now apparent to you which area needs some attention. Perhaps you don't feel you have enough leisure time or have pressing problems involving the care of elderly relatives. Wherever your problems or concerns lie, there will be things you can do to improve your life in your 50s. In this very important decade of your life, you will, no doubt, encounter problems (or you may even have problems left over from your 40s that you have not yet conquered) but as a woman entering this rewarding and challenging phase of your life, you will find solutions.

However, it is obvious that you will not be able to concentrate on too many areas of your life at once, so you must choose the aspect where you will be placing the emphasis and effort. It's your life and only you can choose what you want to improve. Go through some of the lists that you will have prepared for yourself while you've been reading this book and completing the action plans that were important to you, and it will become obvious where you need to put the effort in. Choose to do something that will make an immediate difference to your life so that you can see quick results. You can concentrate on the more difficult areas later. For now, you just need to see a change, so that you can prove to yourself that positive change is possible for you in your 50s.

If it is not absolutely clear to you just where you should start to make improvements in your life and where you will see the greatest benefit, try preparing a life chart as described in the next section.

Completing your life chart

This is a simple, quick, but very rewarding exercise aimed at finding the areas of your life that need attention. The idea is to make a bar chart rating the different aspects of your life. Figure 1 overleaf is an example.

As you can see, each column in the chart represents a specific area of a person's life and a score has been given to each of the life areas to show the level of satisfaction with each. This chart belongs to someone who has had health problems and perhaps has come to a difficult patch with her parents. The chart shows a good relationship with her children but no score in the area of grandchildren – she doesn't have any. The areas of finances, work and relationship all receive good scores but leisure receives a slightly lower one. This person is, overall, happy with her life but needs to do what she can to improve things in regard to her health and her parents. Perhaps she could have a thorough health check and then make improvements to her diet, exercise and lifestyle that would help. There are changes in all these

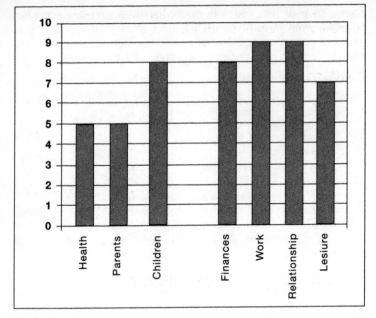

figure 1 life chart

things that would improve health problems such as high cholesterol, diabetes, being overweight, heart disease, skin problems and so on. Of course, it is impossible to change or overcome some health problems but looking after your diet and exercise regime, stopping smoking and cutting alcohol, salt and sugar consumption can all make the small changes that will produce a big difference to how you feel about your health. If you are doing everything you possibly can to help yourself in the face of serious health problems, then you will probably feel better psychologically too.

This person also needs to improve in the area of 'Parents' and maybe this is a temporary problem or there may be issues to resolve. The idea is that the chart will highlight where levels of satisfaction are lowest so that you can then work to improve them. In the area of grandchildren, there is obviously nothing that can be done, but acknowledging that this is a gap in her life will maybe allow this person to look to nephews and nieces or godchildren for the satisfaction that can be gained from close, nurturing relationships with children. Alternatively, she could throw herself into her leisure time, developing new interests and friends, as this is an area where some improvement is possible.

Complete your own chart and see where improvement is needed to make your life fully satisfying.

Summary

This chapter of the book has been all about assessing the different areas of your life and then setting about improving the areas that need it, pulling together the different strands of this book. Becoming familiar with any challenges you have, prioritising them and then working out the action you can take is essential to your happiness now and in the future. Accepting problems as a necessary part of your life, viewing them as challenges and then getting on with your life in a positive frame of mind will help you to enjoy your 50s – even more than your 40s or 30s – and you'll be setting the scene for your 60s and beyond.

Action plan: where to now?

Pick just one area of your life and give it your best shot. Conduct a full review of what you have found out about yourself and the people and activities in your life, using the life chart as described above plus the action plans you will have completed during the course of this book. You should also give yourself plenty of quiet time to reflect on where your life is going and what you want from it. When you have got your thoughts in order, select the area for action and then work out just what you can do about it. Analyse the problems with it – the reasons for your dissatisfaction – and find solutions. Be confident that no problems are without some level of solution. Even if you are stuck with a health condition or are unable to give up a boring job, there will always be something you can do to make improvements. Changing your attitude to the problem often makes it easier to cope with or making the small, daily changes to how you deal with a boring job or health condition will help. There is always something that you can do to help yourself, so do it and start to get more out of your life.

taking it further

Useful organisations and websites

Government departments and websites – general information

Department for Work and Pensions – the part responsible for strategy and policies to support people making decisions about working and retirement. The Age Positive campaign promotes the benefits of employing a mixed-age workforce.

Age Positive Team, Department for Work and Pensions, Room W8d, Moorfoot, Sheffield S1 4PQ
www.agepositive.gov.uk

Information from the government affecting the over 50s
www.direct.gov.uk/Over50s

Department of Social Security, RDFA Unit, Room 37D, Newcastle-upon-Tyne NE98 1YX
www.dss.gov.uk

Department for Education and Skills – the website includes information and advice for adult learners.
www.dfes.gov.uk

Advice on job seeking and benefits

New Deal Information Line
Tel: 0845 6062626

Jobseeker Direct
Tel: 0845 6060234
www.jobcentreplus.gov.uk

Information about pensions

The Pension Service – part of the Department for Work and Pensions. Its free guides to all aspects of state pension schemes can be ordered online.
Tel: 0845 731 3233

www.thepensionservice.gov.uk

The Pensions Advisory Service – offers free information and guidance on state and personal pension schemes.
Tel: 0845 601 2923

www.pensionsadvisoryservice.org.uk

The Pensions Ombudsman – can investigate complaints about occupational schemes.

www.pensions-ombudsman.org.uk

The Financial Ombudsman – can deal with complaints about personal and stakeholder pensions.

www.financial-ombudsman.org.uk

Business Advice

British Chamber of Commerce – the website has links to your local chamber.

www.chamberonline.co.uk

Business Link – the website has links to local Business Link offices.
Tel: 0845 6009006

www.businesslink.gov.uk

Prime – an organisation dedicated to helping people aged 50 or over to set up their own businesses.
PRIME, Astral House, 1268 London Rd, London SW16 4ER
Tel: 0800 783 1904

www.primeinitiative.org.uk

Information about starting a business
www.startups.co.uk

Franchising advice and information

British Franchise Association – a non-profit making body responsible for developing and promoting fair and ethical franchising.
www.british-franchise.org.uk

General advice about starting a franchise
www.whichfranchise.com

Banks

Lloyds TSB Bank
www.lloydstsb.com

Royal Bank of Scotland
www.rbs.co.uk

HSBC bank
www.hsbc.co.uk

First Direct – online bank, part of HSBC
www.firstdirect.com

Natwest Bank
www.natwest.com

Co-operative bank
www.co-operativebank.co.uk

Barclay's bank
www.barclays.com

Abbey business banking
www.anbusiness.com

General Help and Advice

Citizens Advice Bureau
www.citizensadvice.org.uk

Age Concern in England
www.ageconcern.org.uk

Age Concern Scotland
www.ageconcernscotland.org.uk

Age Concern Northern Ireland
www.ageconcernni.org

Age Concern Wales
www.accymru.org.uk

Help the Aged organisation
www.helptheaged.org.uk

Association of Retired and Persons Over 50, Windsor House, 1270 London Road, London SW16 4DH
Tel: 020 8764 3344
www.arp050.org.uk

Website with information for over 50s
www.seniority.co.uk

Website with lots of information about work/life balance in your 50s
www.fiftyon.co.uk

Plenty of information about enjoying later life
www.laterlife.com

National Association of Estate Agents – can help with buying property both in the UK and abroad.
www.naea.co.uk

Directory of dating agencies with ratings and tips
www.dating-agencies-uk.co.uk

Redundancy

Information about redundancy
www.redundancyhelp.co.uk

Learning

Learndirect – an ideal place to start your research on training or to get careers advice.
Tel 0800 100 900
www.learndirect.co.uk

City and Guilds – information about their qualifications
www.city-and-guilds.co.uk

University of the Third Age – a nationwide organisation for retired people who want to learn new skills and hobbies.
www.u3a.org.uk

Information about courses, with a specific area for older learners
www.lifelonglearning.co.uk

Volunteering

Database of volunteer opportunities that you can search by postcode
www.do-it.org.uk

Information about volunteering
www.volunteering.org.uk

Retired and Senior Volunteer Programme
Tel: 0207 6431385

www.csv-rsvp.org.uk

Voluntary group to clean up the streets of a Cheshire town (started by a resident)
www.middlewich-cleanteam.co.uk

Holidays

Holidays for single people
www.self-improvement-holidays.co.uk

More holidays for singles
www.solosholidays.co.uk

Health Information

The Alzheimer's Society, Gordon House, 10 Greencoat Place, London SW1P 1PH
Helpline: 0845 300 0336 (8 a.m. to 6 p.m.)
Tel: 020 7306 0606
www.alzheimers.org.uk

Cancer Research UK – organisation with extensive information about breast cancer.
www.cancerresearchuk.org

Breast Cancer Care – information and support for people affected by breast cancer.
www.breastcancercare.org.uk

Information on managing the menopause
www.menopausematters.co.uk

Further reading

Menopause

Menopause at your Fingertips by Dr Heather Currie (Class Publishing, June 2006)

The New Natural Alternatives to HRT by Dr Marilyn Glenville (Kyle Cathie, January 2003)

The Wisdom of Menopause by Dr Christiane Northrup (Piatkus, April 2001)

Employment

Teach Yourself Flexible Working by Carol Elston and Sue Orrell (Hodder Education, June 2005)

Teach Yourself Managing Your Own Career by Pat Scudamore and Hilton Catt (Hodder Education, January 2003)

Starting a business

Business Plans in a Week by Iain Maitland (Hodder Arnold, October 2002)

Teach Yourself Business Plans by Polly Bird (Hodder Education, November 2004)

Teach Yourself Setting up a Small Business by Vera Hughes and David Weller (Hodder Education, January 2003)

The Small Business Start-up Workbook by Cheryl D. Rickman and Dame Anita Roddick (How To Books, May 2005)

Teach Yourself Franchising by Kurt Illetschko (Hodder Education, May 2006)

Teach Yourself Running Your Own Business by Kevin Duncan (Hodder Education, January 2005)

Decluttering

Teach Yourself Decluttering by Bernice Walmsley (Hodder Education, December 2005)

index

From Advanced Sudoku to Zulu, you'll find everything you need in the **teach yourself** range, in books, on CD and on DVD.

Visit **www.teachyourself.co.uk** for more details.

Advanced Sudoku and Kakuro
Afrikaans
Alexander Technique
Algebra
Ancient Greek
Applied Psychology
Arabic
Aromatherapy
Art History
Astrology
Astronomy
AutoCAD 2004
AutoCAD 2007
Ayurveda
Baby Massage and Yoga
Baby Signing
Baby Sleep
Bach Flower Remedies
Backgammon
Ballroom Dancing
Basic Accounting
Basic Computer Skills
Basic Mathematics
Beauty
Beekeeping
Beginner's Arabic Script
Beginner's Chinese Script
Beginner's Dutch

Beginner's French
Beginner's German
Beginner's Greek
Beginner's Greek Script
Beginner's Hindi
Beginner's Italian
Beginner's Japanese
Beginner's Japanese Script
Beginner's Latin
Beginner's Mandarin Chinese
Beginner's Portuguese
Beginner's Russian
Beginner's Russian Script
Beginner's Spanish
Beginner's Turkish
Beginner's Urdu Script
Bengali
Better Bridge
Better Chess
Better Driving
Better Handwriting
Biblical Hebrew
Biology
Birdwatching
Blogging
Body Language
Book Keeping
Brazilian Portuguese

Bridge
British Empire, The
British Monarchy from Henry VIII, The
Buddhism
Bulgarian
Business Chinese
Business French
Business Japanese
Business Plans
Business Spanish
Business Studies
Buying a Home in France
Buying a Home in Italy
Buying a Home in Portugal
Buying a Home in Spain
C++
Calculus
Calligraphy
Cantonese
Car Buying and Maintenance
Card Games
Catalan
Chess
Chi Kung
Chinese Medicine
Christianity
Classical Music
Coaching
Cold War, The
Collecting
Computing for the Over 50s
Consulting
Copywriting
Correct English
Counselling
Creative Writing
Cricket
Croatian
Crystal Healing
CVs
Czech
Danish
Decluttering
Desktop Publishing
Detox

Digital Home Movie Making
Digital Photography
Dog Training
Drawing
Dream Interpretation
Dutch
Dutch Conversation
Dutch Dictionary
Dutch Grammar
Eastern Philosophy
Electronics
English as a Foreign Language
English for International Business
English Grammar
English Grammar as a Foreign Language
English Vocabulary
Entrepreneurship
Estonian
Ethics
Excel 2003
Feng Shui
Film Making
Film Studies
Finance for Non-Financial Managers
Finnish
First World War, The
Fitness
Flash 8
Flash MX
Flexible Working
Flirting
Flower Arranging
Franchising
French
French Conversation
French Dictionary
French Grammar
French Phrasebook
French Starter Kit
French Verbs
French Vocabulary
Freud
Gaelic

Gardening
Genetics
Geology
German
German Conversation
German Grammar
German Phrasebook
German Verbs
German Vocabulary
Globalization
Go
Golf
Good Study Skills
Great Sex
Greek
Greek Conversation
Greek Phrasebook
Growing Your Business
Guitar
Gulf Arabic
Hand Reflexology
Hausa
Herbal Medicine
Hieroglyphics
Hindi
Hindi Conversation
Hinduism
History of Ireland, The
Home PC Maintenance and
  Networking
How to DJ
How to Run a Marathon
How to Win at Casino Games
How to Win at Horse Racing
How to Win at Online Gambling
How to Win at Poker
How to Write a Blockbuster
Human Anatomy & Physiology
Hungarian
Icelandic
Improve Your French
Improve Your German
Improve Your Italian
Improve Your Spanish
Improving Your Employability

Indian Head Massage
Indonesian
Instant French
Instant German
Instant Greek
Instant Italian
Instant Japanese
Instant Portuguese
Instant Russian
Instant Spanish
Internet, The
Irish
Irish Conversation
Irish Grammar
Islam
Italian
Italian Conversation
Italian Grammar
Italian Phrasebook
Italian Starter Kit
Italian Verbs
Italian Vocabulary
Japanese
Japanese Conversation
Java
JavaScript
Jazz
Jewellery Making
Judaism
Jung
Kama Sutra, The
Keeping Aquarium Fish
Keeping Pigs
Keeping Poultry
Keeping a Rabbit
Knitting
Korean
Latin
Latin American Spanish
Latin Dictionary
Latin Grammar
Latvian
Letter Writing Skills
Life at 50: For Men
Life at 50: For Women

Life Coaching
Linguistics
LINUX
Lithuanian
Magic
Mahjong
Malay
Managing Stress
Managing Your Own Career
Mandarin Chinese
Mandarin Chinese Conversation
Marketing
Marx
Massage
Mathematics
Meditation
Middle East Since 1945, The
Modern China
Modern Hebrew
Modern Persian
Mosaics
Music Theory
Mussolini's Italy
Nazi Germany
Negotiating
Nepali
New Testament Greek
NLP
Norwegian
Norwegian Conversation
Old English
One-Day French
One-Day French – the DVD
One-Day German
One-Day Greek
One-Day Italian
One-Day Portuguese
One-Day Spanish
One-Day Spanish – the DVD
Origami
Owning a Cat
Owning a Horse
Panjabi
PC Networking for Small
  Businesses

Personal Safety and Self
  Defence
Philosophy
Philosophy of Mind
Philosophy of Religion
Photography
Photoshop
PHP with MySQL
Physics
Piano
Pilates
Planning Your Wedding
Polish
Polish Conversation
Politics
Portuguese
Portuguese Conversation
Portuguese Grammar
Portuguese Phrasebook
Postmodernism
Pottery
PowerPoint 2003
PR
Project Management
Psychology
Quick Fix French Grammar
Quick Fix German Grammar
Quick Fix Italian Grammar
Quick Fix Spanish Grammar
Quick Fix: Access 2002
Quick Fix: Excel 2000
Quick Fix: Excel 2002
Quick Fix: HTML
Quick Fix: Windows XP
Quick Fix: Word
Quilting
Recruitment
Reflexology
Reiki
Relaxation
Retaining Staff
Romanian
Running Your Own Business
Russian
Russian Conversation

teach
yourself

managing stress
terry looker & olga gregson

- Do you want to understand the theory behind managing stress?
- Do you want to identify the sources of stress in your life?
- Are you looking for your own stress management plan?

Managing Stress is a step-by-step guide to dealing with stress, leading to a healthier, more relaxed and enjoyable way of life. The questionnaire to assess your stress levels will enable you to identify the signs, symptoms and sources of stress. You will understand what is happening to you mentally and physically and you will learn coping strategies to bring balance to your life.

Professor Terry Looker and **Dr Olga Gregson** are Fellows of the International Stress Management Association. They lecture at the Manchester Metropolitan University and worldwide and present stress management programmes for industry and the professions.

teach yourself	**fitness** jeff archer

- Do you want to learn how to get fit?
- Do you need to know how to make exercise part of daily life?
- Would you like to set and reach physical goals?

Can't find the time to get fit? Don't know where to start? **Fitness** will show you how to formulate, set and stick to a realistic exercise routine, whatever your age or ability. Covering everything from staying motivated to eating sensibly and avoiding injury, this book will help you stay fit with or without a gym, and even with the family. Featuring exercises, information, tips and tricks, this is all you need to get fit and stay that way.

Jeff Archer is a personal trainer and life coach, and a founder and director of The Tonic, a lifestyle and fitness consultancy – www.the-tonic.com.

life coach
jeff archer

- Do you need your life overhauled?
- Would you like to be satisfied at work and home?
- Do you want strategies for long-term success?

If you've ever wanted to boost your confidence and set yourself new goals, **Life Coach** is for you. It gives you direct, friendly motivation to review your aims, challenge your negative beliefs, and achieve fulfilment in all areas. It also provides checklists case studies and all the practical resources you need to get where you want to be professionally, personally, physically and financially.

Jeff Archer is a coach and director at Upgrade My Life, a life coaching consultancy that works with individuals and organizations helping them to reach peak performance. He is a regular contributor to a wide range of national media, newspapers and magazines.

life at 50 – for men
robert ashton

- Are you a man turning 50 or there already?
- Are you wanting to set new goals?
- Do you want to seize fresh opportunities?

Are you a man turned or about to turn 50? This decade offers a whole new range of personal and professional opportunities. **Life at 50** shows how your unique combination of experience and flexibility will help you set new goals from keeping fit to avoiding ageism at work. Packed with checklists and case studies, this book will help you turn your life around.

Robert Ashton is a writer, entrepreneur and business consultant. He is the author of several successful business books, and writes for many popular publications.

ayurveda

teach yourself

sarah lie

- Do you want to understand this ancient Indian tradition?
- Would you like to know your mind and body type?
- Do you want guidance on diet and detox?

Ayurveda is designed to help you maximise the spiritual and physical benefits of an ancient Indian tradition, from understanding your 'type' to finding out about the principles behind illness. It will explain how to construct a diet that works for you, follow an effective detox programme, and suggest useful self-healing strategies. It introduces the herbs and spices of ayurveda, and gives plenty of helpful resources such as recipes, a glossary and a guide to practitioners.

Sarah Lie is journalist, writer and qualified practitioner of ayurveda medicine who carried out her clinical training in India.

reflexology
chris stormer

- Would you like to enjoy the benefits of foot message?
- Do you want to discover the links between mind and body?
- Are you keen to relieve your tension and improve your health?

Reflexology is an ancient and gentle form of healing that uses reflexes on the feet to increase energy and improve wellbeing, mentally, emotionally and spirituality. Fully updated and packed with new resources and user-friendly information. Reflexology will make sure that you get the most out of this soothing art.

Chris Stormer has worked in the complementary health field for 15 years and is an acknowledges authority on reflexology. She is founder and president of the Academy of University Health and Healing and presents workshops worldwide.

teach yourself

massage
denise whichello brown

- Are you interested in the benefits of massage?
- Do you want to learn a variety of techniques?
- Would you like to know about oils and different kinds of massage?

Massage introduces both the practical skills and the spiritual principles behind an ancient and highly influential practice. Follow this illustrated guide to learn about everything from stress relief, treating sports injuries and self-massage, to using massage in relationships and while pregnant. This new edition includes even more practical advice and medical background, as well as fully updated resources and information.

Denise Whichello Brown is a highly acclaimed practitioner, lecturer and author of international repute, with over 20 years' experience in complementary medicine.

yoga
mary stewart

- Are you interested in the origins and history of yoga?
- Do you want to find if yoga might be right for you?
- Would you like to make it part of your everyday life?

Yoga explains both the theory and practice of yoga. With clear, step-by-step illustrations it explains yoga breathing and meditation and shows you how to perform the poses, to promote flexibility and strength and relieve the stress of everyday living. Find out how this ancient system of meditation and exercise can transform your life!

Mary Stewart has been teaching yoga for over 30 years and is the author of five books on the subject.

teach yourself

aromatherapy
denise whichello brown

- Do you want to enjoy the enormous benefits of aromatherapy?
- Do you want to understand the basic principles?
- Do you need help finding the right oils for you?

Aromatherapy is a complete guide to an ancient and popular technique used to treat a wide range of ailments. It gives detailed information on a variety of carrier oils and explores the physical, emotional and spiritual effects of more than 50 essential oils. It also explains techniques for using oils safely and effectively in all areas of your life, including pregnancy and childbirth.

Denise Whichello Brown is a highly acclaimed practitioner, lecturer and author of international repute, with over 20 years' experience in complementary medicine. Foreword by Dr. Joan Kinder, MA, MB, B.Chair(Cantab), MRCP, FRCPCH.

teach
yourself

writing a novel
nigel watts

- Do you want to turn your ideas into a novel?
- Do you need to overcome writer's block?
- Are you looking for advice on getting published?

Writing a Novel takes you through the whole process of writing a novel, from the germ of an idea, through developing plot, character and theme, to preparing it for publication. This fascinating analysis will appeal to both new and experienced authors alike.

Nigel Watts, PhD in Creative and Critical Writing, taught from 1989, the year in which he published his first award-winning novel, *The Life Game*. He went on to publish four further novels for adults, two children's stories and an anthology of spiritual poetry.